D1625317

Golfing in the Zone

Merging Mind, Body, and Spirit Through Golf

Larry Miller

MJF BOOKS

NEW YORK

Published by MJF Books
Fine Communications
Two Lincoln Square
60 West 66th Street
New York, NY 10023

Golfing in the Zone
Library of Congress Card #00-130535
ISBN 1-56731-379-5

Copyright © 1996 by Larry Miller

This edition published by arrangement with Stillpoint Publishing

This book has also been published as *Beyond Golf.*

Text design by Heather Gendron

Manufactured in the United States of America on acid-free paper

MJF Books and the MJF colophon are trademarks of Fine Creative Media, Inc.

10   9   8   7   6   5   4   3   2   1

Dedication

This book is dedicated to my three sons—
Ryan, Jeffrey, and Jonathan.

May your eyes sparkle with curiosity,
Your souls encounter enlightenment,
And your hearts beat with enchantment.

Contents

Acknowledgments

Many people, in many ways, contributed to the conception and production of *Beyond Golf*. Michael Murphy, whom I consider my main mentor in matters concerning the mind-body connection, broadened my view and deepened my understanding of the game's vast hidden meanings. His lessons have amplified, clarified, and explained all of the things I've felt, thought, done, and seen on golf courses and practice tees all over the world for the past forty years. Michael says that his book, *Golf in the Kingdom*, was channeled. Now I understand. So, too, was much of this work. For his *darshan*, his "passing of the light," I am thankful. But I especially thank him for igniting my desire to pursue the openings that led me toward the path of mastery and human potential.

Steve Cohen, president of the Shivas Irons Society, has been a loyal supporter and friend. Steve's sincerity and genuine love and concern for his fellow man set him apart from the ordinary. Indeed, his work is inspiringly extraordinary.

Steve's golf teacher, Fred Shoemaker, author of *Extraordinary Golf*, runs the School for Extraordinary Golf in Carmel, California. Fred's creative curiosity, enthusiasm, and love for the game take me back to when I first started to play golf. His philosophy is filled with that rare sense of innocent joy—that same sense of wonder that filled my early years.

Martin Sage, Gigi, and the entire staff of Sage Productions were inspirational and instrumental in the creation of this work. The Sage Learning Method has enhanced my life and my work.

Meredith Young-Sowers and her magnificent staff at Stillpoint are prime examples of the human creative genius. And they are among the finest and most talented groups of people that I've ever been associated with, in any field.

Special thanks also to Claire Gerus and Anne Sellaro of Stillpoint, who enthusiastically and tirelessly steered this project from the editorial to the marketing stages. Their perception and intuition are unerring.

To Gary Lahoda of Los Angeles, whose editorial and organizational talents—not to mention his great intuitive sense—greatly enhanced this work, I owe a huge debt of gratitude. What a bonus to have an associate who fully understands your work.

I thank Tony Roberts for his hauntingly beautiful cover photo of the fifteenth hole at Machrihanish, in Campbeltown, Scotland. That photo, to me, speaks volumes without a single word.

And of course I thank my entire family for their constant encouragement. Home is such a warm, comfortable place.

As always, a most special thanks to Connie, whose energy and light and insightful daily feedback fuel my fascination for my work and for my life.

Finally, I want to acknowledge all the daring souls out there who choose Love as they seek change. Their positive energies transcend time and space and ripple through all of us.

Foreword

Both scoring and enjoyment in golf depend upon one's mental state and the virtues one brings to the game. More and more golfers, both amateur and professional, are coming to appreciate the fact that golf is as much a spiritual game as it is a physical game.

A few teachers are leading the way to this recognition, among them Larry Miller, who has taught the game in many parts of America and around the world and who has played the PGA Tour. For several years, he has been a pioneering researcher of the inner game. Having watched him teach, I can vouch for both his philosophy and his practical instruction.

Larry helps us see that we encounter all of ourselves when we play, including the farther reaches of our minds. He's good at showing that golf depends upon certain virtues as much as it depends on mechanical expertise. And he helps us understand the mysterious relationships of body and soul, both in sports and in life in general.

Beyond Golf is a wonderful presentation of Larry's philosophy and his methods.

—*Michael Murphy*

Introduction

Golf has been called "the game of a lifetime"—and for good reason. It can be played from ages five to one hundred; it's a healthful game, played outdoors in clean air; and it offers moderate exercise. It's also fun and personally challenging.

Yet, as I pointed out in my previous book, *Holographic Golf,* many golfers don't really enjoy the game. In fact, scores of people who come to the course for relaxation end up going home frustrated and angry—and with shattered self-esteem. The classic love-hate relationship between golfers and their game can become a continuing roller coaster of emotion featuring an abundance of lows, especially if one's expectations are high! Countless marriages, friendships, and business relationships have been destroyed by the game, directly or indirectly. And yet, rare is the divorce from golf!

Why do we players keep coming back? I believe it's because of golf's incredible potential to transform us for the better; the game is filled with an endless supply of powerful, life-enhancing qualities we can tap into. How we can apply golf's transformational potential to our lives is the focus of this book.

Holographic Golf introduced the most effective teaching methods I've learned in more than forty years of playing and teaching the game. Near the end of the book, I began to explore the mental side of golf, which can powerfully increase a player's mechanical effectiveness.

Beyond Golf will take you a significant step farther. This book reveals the many spiritual connections I've discovered in the game. I've learned that the spiritual side of golf can influence the mental side, which influences the physical/mechanical side. The lessons you can learn by viewing golf as a transformative, contemplative discipline can not only improve your golf game, but can profoundly transform your life, as well.

Do we need transformation? To answer, I'd like to quote my friend and mentor, Michael Murphy:

> *"I look around and see a wilderness of broken hearts out there. But if we knew the joy we could find by living fully in our minds and bodies, and if we lived in a culture that encouraged us in contemplative practices, we wouldn't need Prozac. The winds of grace are always blowing, but you've got to raise the sail."*

This book will help you raise your sail and capture those winds of grace. It will explore in a variety of ways the what, the how, and the why of golf's mystical and practical powers. You'll learn how we, as individuals and as a society, can tap into its many strengths. Each of us will also find truths in the game that will raise our awareness and help us to recognize simple daily miracles as they occur.

An inherent part of the game is a set of virtues that mirrors all the qualities desirable in society: integrity, honor, respect, rules, and discipline, to name a few. By exploring these virtues and applying them to our lives, I believe we can influence and even reverse negative trends in society.

And now is the time to do it. As we head into a new century, golf is exploding in popularity. People from all walks of life around the world, even in remote regions, are playing the game. There are more than thirty million golfers in the United States alone, and developers of golf courses struggle to keep up with increasing demand.

Golf's life-changing potential is already being tapped for the good of society. I have founded a program in collaboration with the U.S. Department of Education and the Shivas Irons Society that could have a major impact on our youth and hence on society in general. Operation Golfstart (see Appendix II) kicked off with its pilot program in Memphis,

Tennessee in autumn, 1996. The motto of the program takes the form of a question: "How many eleven or twelve-year-old avid golfers do you know who are in trouble?"

The universal answer is, "None!"

The Shivas Irons Society was founded to honor and further the teachings of Shivas Irons, the main character in Michael Murphy's best-selling book, *Golf in the Kingdom*. At this writing, the Society counts more than 3,000 members, including such high-profile celebrity players as Clint Eastwood and Peter Jacobsen.

The Society does much work with the youth of our country, sponsoring programs to expose the game's many teachings to kids across America, and providing scholarships to worthy and devoted students. In the words of its president, Steve Cohen, the Society is dedicated to "the fostering of education through golf and the furthering of the personal and social transformation that the game can bring."

It is my belief—shared by many others—that we are now experiencing strong winds of change in our society. Golf, with its worldwide appeal and its ability to influence the human psyche, can be a major vehicle in increasing the numbers of the enlightened.

In fact, we are beginning to see the joining of many transformative practices, including golf. It is my hope that they will combine to change and strengthen our society.

Golfing in the Zone

In golf—or in life—the journey begins in innocence. Transformation is really about reclaiming that innocence. The poem, "Angel," written by a Russian poet in the early 19th century, is a beautiful portrayal of the immortality of our perfect and innocent souls. Whenever I read it, I find great comfort. I also give copies of it to all my friends—to lift them up when they're down.

This poem reminds us that there's another "one" within us, one that we can walk with through life as a "perfect twosome."

ANGEL

An angel flew through the midnight sky,
softly singing.
Moon, stars, clouds in a throng
listened to his holy song.

He sang of the bliss of innocent spirits
sinless in paradise.
He sang of the great God,
his praise was unfeigned.

In his arms he bore a young soul,
destined for the world of sorrow and tears.
And the sound of his song stayed forever
wordless and alive in that young soul.

Long that soul languished in the world
filled with a wonderful longing.
The earth's dull songs could not replace
the sounds of heaven for it.

— Mikhail Lermontov
1814-1841

In the present there are no regrets as there are in the past. By thinking of the future you dilute the present. The time to live is now.

—Master Bong Soo Han
Korean martial artist

1

The Perfect Twosome

The game of golf—which encourages introspection and involves our senses and our emotions—can set the stage for inner transformation. The following story illustrates this process, a process we all have the choice to begin. All we may need is a catalyst.

It is said that "when the student is ready, the master appears." Sometimes, the master takes surprising form!

It was one of those picture-perfect, early spring mornings that can turn a golf course into a kind of paradise. Throw in Pebble Beach and you're definitely in Heaven.

Jeffrey Jon Ryan, forty-five, was on vacation. Better yet, it was a golfing vacation. His wife, Debbie, was sleeping in at the lodge and would soon awaken to a sumptuous breakfast and a spectacular view of the Pacific. Her day would be filled with shopping and touring until early evening, when the Ryans had reservations for a sunset dinner at The Old Bath House, a quaint dining hideaway tucked into the cliffs of Pacific Grove, overlooking Monterey Bay.

The Ryans desperately needed this vacation, for the last few years had been rough on their marriage.

Forty-two-year-old Debbie Ryan was a jogger who kept in shape and played an occasional round of golf, if only to appease her husband. Since she'd rather shop and sightsee any day, they would both get their fill of pleasurable activity on this trip. Debbie had brought her golf clubs along and would join Jeff for a round at Spanish Bay later in the week.

Tomorrow, Tuesday, they would drive down the coast highway and visit Nepenthe, the old hippie hangout of the sixties, and take in the majestic splendor of Big Sur. This would be the perfect trip— Jeff's and Debbie's favorite urges would be satisfied in a setting just made for romantic therapy.

Jeff was more than ready for this change of scenery. As a stockbroker for one of Chicago's largest investment firms, he was earning a sizable income. But Jeff had paid dearly for his large income in many ways. Workdays of at least ten hours, constant meetings and seminars, and travel that cut into his weekends made Jeff's job the focal point of his life.

The situation, while making the Ryans' lives financially secure, had taken its toll on the marriage and on family relationships. The couple had attended counseling—despite Jeff's reluctance—and had even endured a brief separation, but the marriage still hung by a thread. This trip was a desperate attempt to reignite the romance, or, at the least, to temporarily adjust the course of the runaway train that their marriage had become.

In the beginning, everything had been fun. Jon Ryan had been a senior, and Debbie McClain a freshman, at Northwestern University. He had been captain of the golf team for the last two years of college and had even entertained thoughts of playing the game professionally. But Jon had always been honest with himself, and he knew that he probably lacked the talent for immediate success. He finally opted for a surer bet: he would become a money expert, and play amateur golf for fun. That way, he could stay close to the game he loved while achieving financial security.

Jon had been good at most sports as a youngster but had quickly gravitated to golf at around age ten. By the time he was fifteen, he was playing golf exclusively and had won a number of junior tournaments. To no one's surprise, he received a scholarship offer from Northwestern, which he accepted.

Debbie McClain was a dark-haired, green-eyed southern belle. Raised in New Orleans society by her French mother and Irish father, Debbie grew up in a warm, proper atmosphere. Yet she dreamed of other places, other ways of life. She yearned to follow the adventurer in her soul.

Her older cousin had enjoyed attending Northwestern in Chicago and Debbie thought that going to an out-of-state school would expand her horizons. She was accepted, and left for Chicago with a wide-eyed anticipation matched only by her southern beauty.

It didn't take long for Jon Ryan and Debbie McClain to find each other. In one of those wild synchronicities that seem to steer our lives, Debbie met Jon while he was student instructing a beginners' golf class. Debbie's father had played golf three to four times a week back in New Orleans, and she had always hated the game. It was too slow, she said. But here she was in college in Chicago, learning golf!

Jon Ryan, tanned, good-looking, intelligent, and friendly, immediately piqued Debbie's interest. Suddenly, she loved the game of golf!

Jon was staggered by Debbie's warm, southern charm and was captivated by her quiet elegance and her enthusiasm for golf.

When they had first started dating, Jeff would sit mesmerized, listening with awe as Debbie expressed herself with simple honesty and deep intuition.

Sometimes, when they'd walked along the shores of Lake Michigan, Debbie would become the teacher and Jeff the student as she described their future together, seeing the changes that awaited them farther on.

They became inseparable, and it soon became apparent that Debbie would never finish college. They were married in New Orleans six months after Jon's graduation. The reception was held at Mr. McClain's country club one day after Jon had consolidated his relationship with his new father-in-law by shooting even par, helping Dad win a few dollars from his golfing buddies.

The couple honeymooned in Europe (including, of course, a brief visit to St. Andrews) before settling down to married life in the affluent northern suburbs of Chicago.

Jon had landed a promising position with a prestigious securities firm and he set about learning all the nuances of handling other people's money. Debbie was equally busy furnishing their new home adjacent to a golf course and teaching aerobics at the health club near their home.

The couple was in such a state of bliss, they scarcely noticed Jon's ten-and eleven-hour workdays. Soon he was taking training seminars on weekends, and he occasionally had to go out of town. But neither he nor Debbie minded because it was all brand new, part of his ascent to the top of the corporate ladder. Debbie even thought Jon's name change to "Jeffrey J. Ryan" for business purposes was cute, and she affectionately dubbed him "Jeffie."

Jeff Ryan was making money and earning promotions, but with each step up he gave up a step at home. When he did get free time, he played golf with clients or colleagues from the firm.

Debbie had begun to be keenly aware of Jeff's 50-60 hour work weeks and weekend golf games, which soon took up three-quarters of the day. Her husband was becoming conspicuous by his absence. In time, though Debbie still dabbled in the game to spend time with Jeff, she began to rediscover her distaste for golf.

Jeff, on the other hand, noticed that Debbie complained a lot, and seemed overly critical of his social drinking. At times, he was irritable and "too tired" to go out to dinner or a movie, activities they had enjoyed before Jeff's meteoric rise in the business world.

The first twelve years of their marriage had given the Ryans two children, a boy and a girl, and the rigors of raising the young family had shielded

Jeff and Debbie from the changes that were slowly, but surely, eroding their relationship.

Now, however, Jeff began to dislike the job that for years had consumed most of his available passion. Even his excellent golf game had deteriorated, despite increased playing time. Jeff found himself becoming deeply depressed. Bearing down on age forty, Jeff found that his health, once a beacon of his strength and fitness, had begun to falter. The stress, the depression, the drinking—all contributed to his growing problems.

Debbie, too, was unhappy. She began to periodically visit her folks in New Orleans, but her mom and dad were growing old. Debbie found herself regretting not having finished college. Her once bustling life, with all its promise, had ground to a halt. Formerly a fitness and health food buff, she had abandoned all but her jogging and more and more frequently had started to join Jeff at "cocktail hour" upon his arrival from work. Cocktail hour at the Ryan's usually passed with minimal conversation, with Jeff reading the paper or watching the news, and Debbie trying to extract answers to mundane questions. Debbie was being introduced to the concept of *alone together*.

The couple had now lost sight of all the attractions that had drawn them together. It wasn't that they didn't notice that the gap between them was widening. Debbie had tried to signal her loneliness and boredom.

She had even suggested counseling, but Jeff, mired in the depths of denial, resisted. Finally, after another futile attempt to get Jeff to agree to counseling, Debbie announced that she was going to New Orleans to stay with her parents "for a while."

Jeff, although devastated by Debbie's leaving, could hardly blame her. He knew that the marriage had been suffering. But he had reached a point that twenty years earlier would have seemed impossible— he had no passion, no fascination for anything. It was as if he were on a mission to oblivion.

After a two-week separation and countless telephone conversations, Jeff and Debbie decided to try again. The wake-up call had stirred Jeff, but only long enough, as it turned out, to re-establish the facade of their marriage. The decline continued.

Then, one crisp morning in late winter while leafing through a travel magazine, Debbie had a brilliant idea—a trip to the Monterey Peninsula! She knew that Jeff had always dreamed of playing Pebble Beach. He spoke of it as if it were some sort of golfing shrine at which he would worship, if he ever got there. So she suggested a trip to the Pacific Coast for golf and sightseeing in one of the world's most romantic settings.

She hoped that Jeff's excitement about playing Pebble Beach, added to the romantic setting, would somehow lift the veil from his emotions. She was sure that there, on the cliffs beside the ocean, surrounded by clouds, they would find each other again. Little did she know that it would be another influence, one she could never have imagined, that would lift the veil that for years had concealed from Jeff the direction his life was taking.

Now, as Debbie slept, dreaming of the possibilities the week might hold, Jeff was exploring the grandeur and mystique of Pebble Beach. He had already checked out the windows of the quaint little shops on the way to the pro shop and the first tee area. Now he was on the practice putting green, waiting for his name to be called.

Jeff had signed up for the earliest tee time possible. Since he was a single, there would be little difficulty getting paired up early. It didn't matter to him when or with whom he might play. After all, playing Pebble Beach for the first time is like getting your first glimpse of the Mona Lisa.

At precisely 7:30 A.M., Jeff Ryan was called to the first tee. But as he bent over to collect his putting balls from the practice green, something strange happened. Suddenly, he felt as if he might pass out. Then a warm sensation enveloped him, penetrating his very being. He perceived light, intense and clear, illuminating his surroundings.

Jeff shook his head and took a deep breath. "It's early and I haven't eaten," he told himself, starting for the first tee. "And I'm all keyed up about being here at Pebble." After all, he reasoned, a golfer's first shot at Pebble happens only once. Jeff was also keenly aware of the Pebble Beach tradition—everyone around the area stops what they're doing to watch the tee shots. Many a nervous golfer's stomach has worsened while being scrutinized by this discerning audience!

Jeff was feeling a bit queasy as the starter explained that his playing partner would be a fourteen-year-old junior champion from the Midwest. The boy's father had brought his son to Pebble Beach as part of his golfing education. Since Jeff had signed the starting time sheet as a three handicapper, the starter had considered them a good pairing, one that would move along at a brisk pace and not tie up the course. The folks at Pebble, in light of the tremendous volume of play every day, are very mindful of such things.

Jeff shook the boy's hand and introduced himself but found himself growing vague when he looked at the boy's eyes. Nor did he catch the youngster's name. Jeff figured he'd get it later in the round or check the boy's bag tag for identification. Yet every time Jeff looked at the boy's eyes, he had the strange sensation that he'd seen them somewhere before.

The youngster seemed much more intense and mature than the average fourteen-year-old, and it was obvious that golf, to him, was serious business. But as soon as Jeff was fooled into thinking his playing partner was older, the boy would flash an engaging, almost playful smile and then gaze at the ocean as if he were looking for something far away.

When the boy's opening tee shot split the crisp air and echoed like a rifle fired in a canyon, Jeff knew that this would be no ordinary round. The drive found the right center of the fairway, about 245 yards off the tee.

Jeff's opening salvo was a nervously tight half-swing that produced a short drive (by Jeff's standards). He was satisfied to see it find the fairway not far behind the youngster's ball. As they walked away from the first tee, a heavy mist moved in from the Pacific and enveloped the entire area, shrouding the pair from everyone else.

It was an eerie feeling, and as Jeff caught a glimpse of the flagstick fading in and out of view on the first green, he had to pinch himself to be sure he wasn't dreaming. All Jeff could see was the boy peering through the mist, calculating his distance to the flag.

"I'm letting this situation get to me," Jeff chided himself. "I've got to take control again and show this kid how the game should be played."

Jeff figured he had about 155 yards to the flag, and with the mist hanging heavy, it might play closer to 160. He decided to swing a smooth six iron and play for the middle of the green, since the flag was on the right, behind a bunker. Jeff made a good, relaxed swing compared to his drive, but the mist was heavier than it looked, and the ball came up short, landing just on the front edge of the green.

"Damned mist," Jeff yelled. "I hit it perfect, and I've got an eighty-footer!"

The boy said nothing and rifled a six iron straight at the flag. The ball carried the bunker with room to spare and stopped dead within eight feet of the hole.

"Great shot!" cried Jeff, who could barely see the white ball close to the flag. "What'd you swing?" The boy just said, "Six," and nothing else.

As they walked up to the green, Jeff congratulated his young friend on a courageous shot over the bunker.

"Thanks," the boy said, flashing that engaging, quick smile. Then he stared at Jeff with a serious, piercing look and said, "The mist was heavy and really held the ball up. It's a situation where you want to be aggressive."

Jeff couldn't believe his ears. This fourteen-year-old kid was not only offering fatherly advice but was subtly criticizing Jeff for his conservative play! It was as if he spoke from years of experience, his tone stern and patronizing.

With a mumbled reply, Jeff predictably three-putted and the kid birdied. Suddenly, he decided to take up the gauntlet and put this brash kid in his place.

It had taken only one hole for Jeff's relaxed appreciation of Pebble Beach to turn into an all-too-familiar golf course scene. Jeff felt hostility, anger, and depression begin to well up in his mind and body. The tension was high as the pair walked to the par five second hole.

Jeff found out that the boy would turn fifteen in a few weeks and had played the course a few times already. He had won a number of junior tournaments and was beating most everyone in town back home. He was a good-looking kid, big for his age but not overweight. Although full of energy and very competitive, he was polite and gracious.

On the way to the second tee, the boy asked Jeff if he had noticed the smell of the ocean on the first green. Jeff thought it was odd that a teenager would notice such a thing while birdieing the first hole at Pebble Beach.

But Jeff *had* smelled the ocean, now that he thought about it, and it suddenly brought him back to why he was here: to enjoy the magnificent surroundings and the joy of playing golf on this incredible course.

The pair played two, three, and four in relative silence and solitude, letting the anticipation build. The anticipation, for those who know Pebble Beach, is for what lies ahead after the fifth green.

When you leave five green and approach six tee, a panorama unfolds like no other in golf.

Augusta National has its Amen Corner, and The Old Course at St. Andrews has all that tradition, but nothing anywhere can rival holes six through ten at Pebble Beach. Playing one through five at Pebble is like climbing the steps to a high diving board. It's a prelude—a great one perhaps—but only a prelude to a magnificence rarely experienced. And as you march down the sixth fairway, with the ocean appearing at every turn and the magical scenery unfolding before you, the course takes on a mystical quality. It is so unreal, it fascinates even the world's most experienced players.

As they left the green of the par three fifth, with the boy even par and Jeff two over, the youngster, knowing that this was Jeff's first trip around the course, said, "Brace yourself, Mr. Ryan, here comes Pebble Beach."

Jeff Ryan, standing on the sixth tee, gazed ahead, drinking in the vista unfolding before him: the long fairway, downhill, then uphill, twisting to the right as if reaching for the Pacific, with dramatic cliffs on the right side dropping straight down to the crashing spray of a sea that never sleeps. Standing on tee six, you can see, smell, and feel the special nature of this golf course. And this is only the beginning! The beauty of the course continues to build, reaching a crescendo on the spectacular and mystical eighth, with nine and ten barely managing to bring you down to earth ever so gently.

After their tee shots on the sixth, the boy suddenly confided, "I sure wish my mom were alive to see this." Jeff asked the boy about his mother and learned that she had died of cancer a few years earlier. Jeff had also lost his mother when he was a youngster, and he found himself thinking back to that sorrowful time.

"She would really have appreciated the beauty of this place," the boy continued, "though my dad wouldn't think so. He said that she hated golf. But she would have loved this course."

Debbie suddenly popped into Jeff's mind. How those words applied to her! Yes, Debbie would love this course. She'd probably love to jog around it, he thought affectionately.

Suddenly, Jeff was sorry Debbie wasn't there with him to share his appreciation of this magical spot. He vowed to bring her out to see it later in the week.

As they began to play to the sixth green, the boy seemed pensive, and Jeff marveled again at his insightful comments. He was a sensitive, perceptive, charismatic child with a killer competitive instinct, yet he was mature and level-headed. He was "intelligently aggressive," a rare combination for someone his age.

There was a burning drive in the boy's eyes that surprised Jeff. How odd, he thought, that this adolescent seemed to combine the focus of Ben Hogan with the charisma and flair of Walter Hagen.

Jeff was looking for the seventh tee before he finished putting on the sixth. The seventh is a par three, barely a hundred yards, and can play like a monster hole. The green is small and well-guarded by sand bunkers. Just over the green is rocky shoreline. But what really makes the seventh exceptional is the fact that it juts out into the ocean, and the tee shot is directly into the teeth of the prevailing wind that blows in from the sea.

Touring pros can hit anything from half sand wedge to four iron, depending on the wind, and they'll take par anytime. When you play the seventh, you feel as if you're playing golf on a raft in the ocean. The hole is simply breathtaking.

The boy played first and lofted a pitching wedge into the slight headwind. As the ball rose on its way to the green, the wind suddenly stopped and the ball flew to the back edge, bounced once, and disappeared over the back of the green. The ball didn't make it to the ocean but lodged in thick, tall grass, from where the youngster's pitch barely made it to the green. During all this adversity, the boy retained an unusual serenity, and even three putted with an air of calm acceptance. As they left the green, Jeff consoled him with, "You sure didn't deserve a five there," to which his playing partner replied, "Just playing that hole sort of overshadows whatever score you make." And it was obvious that he meant it.

Jeff once again picked up on how relevant those words were to his own life. It was eerie the way this boy perceived priorities. It was almost as if he'd been sent to reacquaint Jeff with everything he'd lost sight of, including how to enjoy a round of golf.

The boy had obviously picked up the important lessons golf can teach—the discipline, the sacred rules, the etiquette, the sportsmanship and camaraderie, and the joy of communing with Nature. With a wrenching awareness, Jeff saw himself in this boy, the way he had been before he'd become sidetracked by the pitfalls of upward mobility.

Jeff and the boy headed to the eighth tee, each two over par, with the success of the round hinging on the next three holes. If a golfer can stay respectable through the first ten holes at Pebble Beach, chances for a good score are excellent.

As Jeff began to think more about where his life had gone—and where it once had been—a new resolve began to grow. He wanted to return, if possible, to where he had come from, a place where serenity, appreciation, and clear thinking prevailed.

As he embraced this new resolution, he felt a deep sense of peace steal over him, and on the eighth tee, for the first time in years, he felt that old elasticity and rhythm in his golf swing.

On the eighth tee of golf's best par four, Jeff ripped his drive down the right center with one of those smooth, rhythmic swings that features gradual acceleration and an explosion at impact. Jeff hadn't felt that kind of swing in a long time, but it sure felt good. It provided an instant link with his past golfing successes. How he loved this game! Somehow, Jeff knew that his journey back had begun.

Now he felt lighter, more energetic, and the crystalline waters of the Pacific shimmered as they lashed the coastline edging the eighth fairway.

As Jeff again thought of Debbie, a rush of affection shot through him, followed by regret for the deterioration he had allowed in their marriage. He wished again that she were here now, to share this illumination, this moment of rejuvenation.

Jeff was brought back to the course by the young voice coming from his left. "Nice drive, you're in perfect position."

Surveying the shot at hand, Jeff selected a five iron and repeated the swing of his tee shot. The ball rocketed to the green, then floated down like a parachute as it crawled all over the flagstick. It came to rest no more than eighteen inches from the hole. A tap-in birdie at eight, a rare occurrence indeed!

This round of golf had provided an opening, and now the closure had come. Jeff was entering "the zone," that special arena where concentration is pure and all thoughts are positive.

Even the boy was impressed as they played on, and his enthusiastic shouts of "great shot," and "nice putt" became almost rote as Jeff kept his rhythm. Even the *youngster's* timing improved as he fed off Jeff's energy, and they both came to eighteen at one over par.

There was a backup of golfers on eighteen tee while some workmen finished their duties, so Jeff and the boy had a few minutes to converse.

Looking at Jeff earnestly, the youngster said, "I don't know what you found back there on number eight, because I don't have a name for it, but it happens to me all the time. For no apparent reason, my swing will suddenly be just right. I can *feel* the subtleties in my swing, and I know that I'll hit good shots. But then, without warning, the feeling leaves, and no matter what I try, I can't call it up. It just appears and disappears. What do you think? Is it feel, is it swing speed, is it mental?"

Jeff seized the opportunity to be the teacher, and looked at the boy with affection as he considered how he'd posed those same questions years before, when he'd been the same age as this boy.

In fact, the similarities between Jeff's approach to the game as a youth and this boy's attitude on the golf course were so striking, they were almost disconcerting.

"No one ever masters the game," Jeff said with a fatherly air, "but some survive it and ride its highs and lows. You can't fight it too hard, 'cause the energy of the fight will weaken your playing of the game. If there's any secret to surviving the game and achieving something close to your potential, it's staying positive all the time, no matter what. And use *all* of your senses when you play. They feed valuable information to your mind which controls your muscles. I notice you already have good instincts for that. And don't ever lose sight of your priorities, in golf or in life."

Smiling to himself, Jeff added, "And don't forget to trust your intuition."

Jeff suddenly realized the irony of it all. Here he was, lecturing the boy on what the youngster had just unknowingly taught *him!* But then, as Shivas Irons says in *Golf in the Kingdom*, the passing of the light goes from teacher to student. During this round, each had been both.

The boy just nodded with a little half-smile, and Jeff almost had the feeling that his answer had been expected, that he had somehow passed the test.

They stood on eighteen tee, taking it all in. Eighteen at Pebble is the most famous hole in golf—and it never disappoints. Jeff and the boy were a happy pair as they played eighteen in silence, with the crashing of the waves and the calling of the seabirds providing the only sounds. They both birdied the eighteenth from short range, then shook hands in the middle of the green as the fog made an inland move.

Jeff and his companion were literally in the clouds as they walked off, complimenting each other on their even par rounds of seventy-two. "You've got a bright future in golf," Jeff told the boy with sincerity. "I'll be following your career with great interest."

As Jeff moved away from the green, he realized that he didn't even know the boy's name. And yet this stranger had helped him to rediscover his innocence, his joy, and the clarity of thought that accompanies untarnished youth. Jeff knew now that his child within, the child who for so long had been stifled and forgotten, was still alive and well.

Jeff was beginning to realize the impact this round of golf would have on his life, and he wanted to reach back to thank the young man in some way. He was embarrassed that he didn't even know the boy's name.

Suddenly, Jeff stopped and turned back toward the green where the boy still stood, now almost completely hidden by the fog and mist. Jeff could barely make out the boy's outline as he shouted, "Wait! I can't follow your golf career without knowing your name."

The boy said nothing, just stared out at the sea, holding his putter as if it were the sword of some triumphant warrior.

"Who are you?" asked Jeff, as the boy's image began to fade.

An eerie, faraway voice came back through the clouds, as if it were coming from another time and place. "Don't you know me? My name is Jon Ryan, and I am you, thirty years ago. Remember this round whenever you play and when you talk to your wife or your children. And remember, too, that I am within you and will always be part of you. For after all, Jeff, you and I together are *the perfect twosome!*"

Jeff was close to fainting now, feeling that same strange light-headedness he'd experienced right before the round. Again, everything seemed bathed in light.

Suddenly, he heard a loud ringing. Someone was shaking him. It was Debbie, leaning over him, saying, "Wake up, Jeff, you'll be late for your tee time. I can't believe it! It's your first round at Pebble Beach and you've overslept. And you've been smiling in your sleep for the past twenty minutes. It must have been some dream!"

Jeff blinked, caught between two worlds. Then, reaching out, he pulled Debbie close. "I want you to come with me to play Pebble, even if you just walk the course. I want you to experience it with me."

Debbie thought she was hearing things. Tears stung her eyelids. The sincerity and affection in his voice was something she'd never thought she would hear again.

Quickly, Debbie said, "I'd love to. Let's get dressed before you're late. But Jeff, before we leave, tell me what you were dreaming."

Jeff just smiled. It was the same warm, engaging, playful smile that had always been a trademark of Jon Ryan's. Tightening his arms around Debbie, he kissed her and said, "Let's go to Pebble Beach so you can see and feel the magic with me. And then tonight, we'll go to dinner, order two bottles of the best champagne, and I'll tell you all about it."

Remember, Friend, as you pass by,
As you are now, so once was I.
As I am now, so you must be.
Prepare yourself to follow me.

—Anonymous epitaph

2

The Golfer's Inner Journey

There are those who believe that people are unable to change. One phrase we often hear is, "Leopards can't change their spots." And while that statement is probably true about leopards, I believe it's wrong to apply it to human beings.

We can change—and we do.

The problem is, we seldom hear the quiet little success stories like those of the Jeff Ryans of this world. Yet we all have an awesome power to transform ourselves, to change for the better. But we need motivation and a vehicle—a *fascination*—to take us through the doorway that's always there.

The fictional account of Jeff Ryan's journey toward the discovery of what really mattered in his life illustrates that process. Jeff had two strong catalysts for change. First, he had his lifelong love for the game of golf, heightened by the experience of playing one of the world's most celebrated courses, Pebble Beach. He also had the inspiring presence of his mysterious playing partner. These factors combined to prompt his inner awakening, and he was able to uncover the motivation to change that had always been within him, hidden just below the surface.

With his new awareness, Jeff was able to see that he had lost touch with many qualities he admired. First, he relearned how to discover the truth about his life, an ability that had been dimmed by his confusion and depression. As he did so, he was once again able to feel genuine affection for his wife, Debbie.

Second, he learned that succeeding, whether in a round of golf or in life, requires a positive attitude, no matter what happens. And third, he became acutely aware, perhaps for the first time, that there's more to life than making money and winning on the golf course. There's a spiritual dimension, as well.

I have identified "Seven Stages of a Golfer's Spiritual Evolution." You'll be able to recognize where you are on the path, where the journey can take you, and how you can get there.

Stage 1 — The Innocent

In this stage, the golfer is a beginner, new to the game and full of anticipation and excitement. Perhaps parents or friends play, or perhaps business associates provide the impetus to take up the game. Whatever the reason, it's a time when the challenge of the unknown—the game—beckons.

It's also a time when it's fun to play—even if one is playing alone, enjoying Nature, fresh air, and exercise. The game is played without the burden of ego-driven or social pressures. It's a pure form of learning in which everything is brand new and exciting. There is little anger when mistakes or failures occur, only a desire to learn.

But early in the Innocent's infancy, just as in life, a gate opens and in walks *ego*. And what an entrance! Curiosity and wonder are suddenly overwhelmed, although, as we learned in Jeff Ryan's story, the innocence of childhood remains dormant, waiting like Sleeping Beauty to be reawakened.

The Innocent eventually meets other golfers, makes new golfing friends, or develops to the point where peers or business associates issue invitations to play. Suddenly, what was a relaxed, pressure-free period of learning becomes a competitive situation. Now the ego is involved because good shots, or at least acceptable ones, matter. Scores assume a new importance. Soon, anxiety about perceived scrutiny—that feeling of being observed and judged— appears.

Stage 2 — The Frustrated Golfer

Now, the Frustrated Golfer emerges. At this stage, the golfer has hit enough good shots to be able to gauge his or her potential. However, bad shots are still in the majority. So the Frustrated Golfer knows that his or her true potential will not always be apparent. When fears of failure are justified by poor performance, the result is anger, frustration, and humiliation. After enough humiliation, the Frustrated Golfer becomes determined to improve and play better rounds more often. The Achiever is about to be born.

Stage 3 — The Achiever

In the typical scenario, the Frustrated Golfer quickly assumes the characteristics of the Achiever. These include a sudden interest in all forms of instruction—books, magazines, videos, lessons, golf schools, and training aids. The Achiever becomes devoted to practice and self-improvement, under-taking a fervent quest for enough proficiency to be able to play with other, more advanced Achievers. In fact, the desire to gain status among the better players usually fuels this quest for excellence.

This stage can last for many years, and in some ways it never ends. The Achiever's quest, when undertaken as a "practice" on the road to mastery, can be an exciting and fulfilling journey. Every Achiever will find, however, that the initial spark will ultimately fade, just as the honeymoon stage will wane in many relationships. This doesn't signal the end of the love affair, only that the relationship has naturally evolved. And it doesn't mean that the work is over, or even that its intensity has lessened. The Achiever can devote many years' work to reaching ever-deepening levels of understanding in golf, relationships, marriage, and family life.

But eventually, time and maturity will temper the Achiever's driving forces. As available energies begin to appear, they are directed to acts of altruism and graciousness, sure signs of the appearance of the Giver.

Stage 4 — The Giver

The Giver may retain certain characteristics of the Achiever, but as personal evolution continues, the ego shows signs of dissolving. Sooner or later, the Achiever realizes that there is joy and fulfillment to be had in guiding and sharing with others.

A typical example is the hard-driving executive who, after retirement, enjoys taking his boat out early in the morning to teach his grandchild how to fish. He displays all the patience, love, and tenderness one human being can offer another. Quite a contrast to his competitive days in the corporate battle zone.

I've also seen this scenario played out on golf courses and driving ranges all over the world. The Giver often seeks out mentoring situations, especially with youngsters. As a golf professional, I've seen many colleagues suddenly develop a great interest in junior golf. If one practices a fascination long enough, the *passion* for it—and the love of sharing it—eventually radiates outward to those nearby. The Giver receives joy by sharing it with others.

This new level is evident in every aspect of the Giver's life. The giver performs small acts of altruism without fanfare, exercises more patience, and exhibits more spiritual awareness, sometimes surfacing as an increasing interest in religion.

Despite this transformation, the Giver can still aspire to greater heights as a golfer. But there's been a shift, an added dimension that will now enrich the journey. This stage is also marked by less anger and frustration and less of a need to struggle when difficulties arise. The fire still burns within, but its flame is tempered by a knowing acceptance that filters the heat and directs it efficiently and appropriately.

For many golfers, the conscious journey of alchemy ends here, as they continue to aspire to greater heights of performance, while giving of themselves unselfishly and with love. But there are some who choose to analyze and philosophize. These people move up the mountain searching for further enlightenment. They are the Seekers.

Stage 5 —The Seeker

Seekers look for answers and for the higher meaning behind every experience. They see life in an overview, as a broadening picture. They also become aware of golf's inherent virtues and the value of the lessons it can teach. Often, Seekers are lifelong players, real students of the game whose years of practice and study pull the curtains back to reveal previously hidden truths and insights.

Seekers are often fearful of skepticism and ridicule, so they keep their thoughts to themselves and may be difficult to identify. Their studies are conducted in isolation. Seekers still aspire, but the object of their aspirations may change. They use the physical realm as a laboratory in which to study the inner realms. There is no more anger involved with their performances, only inquiry. Seekers analyze and dissect their growth processes.

Stage 6 —The Seer

Sometimes after extensive study, understanding is finally reached. Suddenly, the Seeker sees. The various stages of inner transformation are recognized as part of a whole process, manifesting in the present moment. The mask of the self now comes off and the Seer can identify with all others.

Just how can one determine if there is a Seer dwelling within them? One begins increasingly to experience serendipity, synchronicity, or mere coincidence. If intuition is also involved in this event, then the Seer is at work, recognizing the clues to life's mysteries.

How does one recognize another Seer? It takes one to know one.

Stage 7 — The Spirit-Golfer

It is the Seer who has the best chance of reaching the final stage of evolution where Spirit is the dominating factor. But all golfers can touch a part of Spirit while playing the game. Ram Dass, the noted metaphysical writer who is also a golfer, suggests that we play the game with no attachment to the result. Play golf, he says, "without being the golfer."

Spirit-Golfers don't play the golf course—the golf course plays them. Nature helps them play intuitively, and they are consummate masters of the art of blending. Not only do they recognize and use all available helping currents, they also see themselves as an integral part of the helping currents. To the Spirit-Golfer, the score is simply another reflection of the experience, a reflection from which many lessons can be learned.

And that takes us back to the Innocent, who can play without ego, with only curiosity and awareness.

But what about the rest of us? What about all our acquired baggage: the good shots, the bad shots, the successes and the failures?

The answer lies in pursuing a path that takes us through all the above stages of evolution, using tools we will be discussing in the following chapters. Like Jeff Ryan, we need to prepare for a return to innocence. As we continue to work on our growth, our egos will diminish, and one day we will experience a blending of these stages into that of the wise and innocent Spirit-Golfer—a being who continues to ride the waves of evolution, while reveling in the joy of the present moment.

If you want to learn how to swing a golf club, don't listen to a golf professional—watch him.

—Larry Miller

3

Learning from the Game

We begin learning at birth. As infants, our curiosity is fresh and unquenchable, and as young children, we exhibit a hunger for knowledge. This insatiable, lifelong desire to know things continues as we begin our schooling and follows us into adulthood. As adults, we learn what's going on in our world by talking to each other and letting the media fill in the rest. Even as nations, we seek to learn what's out there beyond our own world by venturing into outer space.

Unfortunately, we've all known people who have lost their curiosity about life. Often, they seem to have lost their zest for life, as well. It's as if the desire for knowledge is a tonic, as well as a vital sign that announces to the world that we're still alive and kicking.

A search for answers was certainly the theme at a golf-writers' conference I attended in Carmel, California, in 1994, along with such noted writers as Michael Bamberger, Lorne Rubenstein, and Jaime Diaz of *Sports Illustrated.* For three days we explored a variety of questions about golf. But the one that kept recurring was, "Why is the game so universally popular?" What, we asked each other, is the mysterious lure of the game that has hooked an estimated 100 million people throughout the world?

Although we kicked around all sorts of theories, we left Carmel without a clear answer. I believe, however, that Michael Murphy, who also attended the conference, came closest to solving the riddle. Murphy suggests that when we find something that "lights us up," we must take every step to pursue it. Nothing is sadder, Murphy goes on, than a person who has no "fascination."

When a child pulls apart an expensive toy, it's because he or she wants to learn how it works. This curiosity, when not easily satisfied, leads us to a deeper level of interest—the level of fascination. Applying this principle to the adult world, it's easy to see how some of our more complex activities, such as golf, can lead to obsessions often lifelong in nature.

Golf can challenge us on so many levels that Murphy refers to the game as a "mystery school." For one thing, no two golf shots are ever alike. The golf course is vast, the target (the hole) is moved daily, no two lies are ever alike, conditions are ever-changing, and no two swings are identical. Even the world's best players, who practice daily to perfect their swings, will admit that they can feel the subtle differences in each swing, even though to observers the swings may appear to be identical.

It's this endless variety of possibilities that makes the game so interesting and invites both curiosity and fascination. Just stand on the practice range and start practicing seven iron shots. Don't change positions and don't change targets. Just keep hitting seven irons, over and over. How long before boredom sets in? Not long, I can assure you.

As you go deeper into practice, you'll ultimately find that no matter how long you try, you can't repeat your "perfect" shots, even if you're willing to practice that seven iron shot for twenty years! But the quest for perfection never ends.

And that inability to master the golf swing can intrigue many of us to the point of real obsession, harmless to some, but destructive to others. Yet, to all who are in relentless pursuit of perfecting the swing, the attraction to achieve this goal never goes away.

Where can this attraction, this *fascination* lead us? And what can we learn from golf?

Our fascination with golf keeps us coming back, despite disappointments. And only by doing so can we take advantage of the many opportunities the game offers us to transform ourselves.

Early on, new players learn that golf is very much an honorable game with time-honored traditions. These traditions are followed by everyone, including die-hard individualists. It has been said that even a common criminal wouldn't consider cheating on a golf course or violating any of golf's sacred rules.

Golf offers a number of virtues—elements of pure goodness. The wise player will recognize, with increasing exposure to the game, that these virtues are a reflection of those within himself or herself. By working with this awareness, the golfer can begin to transform personal weaknesses into strengths, at the same time increasing his or her ability to play the game effectively.

Here are some of the virtues the game can teach:

1. Respect for rules
2. Personal honor and self-discipline
3. Sportsmanship and camaraderie
4. Self-control
5. Responsibility
6. Self-discovery
7. Organized thinking
8. Health benefits
9. Family unity

Let's explore these one by one, so we can see the many opportunities this game offers to help us change our lives for the better.

l. Respect for rules

First, the game teaches us the importance of rules. Golf's rules are the strongest fibers in the fabric of the game. The rules are strictly governed by associations and organizations that have been around for centuries. They are enforced diligently, and the changing or amending of a rule is no small thing. This adherence to a code of conduct helps to preserve the integrity of the game from generation to generation, and every junior clinic or class emphasizes comprehensive coverage of the rules.

2. Personal honor and self-discipline

Golf can be played alone or with others, but even when we're surrounded by others, we're still playing alone. There is no teammate to blame or lean on, and other players are too concerned with their own games to pay attention to whether or not someone else is obeying every rule. Personal honor becomes a part of one's on-course behavior. And together, honoring the rules and exerting self-discipline not only preserve the integrity of the game, they help to build strength of character.

3. Sportsmanship and camaraderie

Two additional positive aspects of human nature the game will inspire are sportsmanship and camaraderie. Professional golf is unique in that it's the only play-for-pay sport in which you'll find competitors actually cheering each other on. When I first played on the PGA Tour, I marveled at how even tough veteran players would sincerely wish good luck to the other players in their group, and applaud the good shots of their playing partners.

Golfers really *do* respect other golfers.

Golfing etiquette is another important aspect of sportsmanship. Even during the most casual outing, golfing etiquette, such as waiting one's turn, is strictly adhered to. I'm often amazed and amused to observe people who disregard politeness in other areas of their lives, yet follow strict golfing etiquette with total strangers in an informal pick-up game!

4. Self-control

A round of golf can truly resemble an emotional roller-coaster ride. Good and bad shots come without warning, and many of us have seen a playing partner shift from a club-throwing maniac to the happiest player on Earth, all in the span of one hole. When the results of our efforts don't meet our expectations, our psyches are dealt a severe blow.

Being able to control disappointment and anger is a major step on the path to self-improvement.

The world's best players strive to maintain an even emotional keel so they can retain their concentration. By practicing this skill we can calm our minds and help develop the mental discipline we'll need for effective play over long stretches of time.

5. Responsibility

There are many things golfers must be responsible for in golf, and neglecting them can lead to poor performance, the last thing any of us wants. As golfers, we're responsible for our equipment, the whereabouts of our golf balls, our scores, our adherence to the rules and etiquette, and our performances. If we have caddies, we're also responsible for the caddies' behavior.

Learning to accept and handle all of these responsibilities will strengthen our confidence as golfers.

6. Self-discovery

The game can teach us volumes about ourselves. It's been said that to really learn about someone, play a round of golf with him or her. Golf can expose a complete cross-section of one's personality during the course of a round, as we've already seen in "The Perfect Twosome."

And if you really want to step back and take a look at yourself, try playing eighteen holes alone, paying close attention to your thoughts, as well as to your performance. Later, when you reflect on your solitary round, you'll be surprised at how many fascinating observations you'll have made about yourself.

Then, compare these with your behavior when playing with friends or strangers. You'll learn that you have many different personalities, depending on who your golfing companions might be.

7. Organized thinking

Golf is a game of great strategy. When we play well, our game can resemble a game of chess or billiards, in which we plan our moves ahead. For this reason, golf can be a great tonic for a disorganized mind. We can learn how to strategize, plan, organize, and weigh many factors at once.

8. Health benefits

Golf is a healthful game played outdoors in an expansive natural setting complete with trees, birds, and other wildlife. It encourages walking, and the continued swinging of the club is a very beneficial moderate exercise. In fact, golf is often prescribed as a rehabilitative activity. What better way to shed the pressures of business or to get away from the asphalt jungle? We can certainly be rejuvenated in both mind and body.

9. Family unity

Once thought of as strictly a "man's game," golf has become popular with all segments of the population. Indeed, for the last 3 years, 60% of all new golfers are women.

In addition, nearly every golf club insists on a strong junior program, where boys and girls aged seven to sixteen learn the fundamentals of the game from PGA professionals.

All of this has resulted in a marked increase in the number of families who play golf together and become exposed, as a family, to the game's powerful teachings and virtues.

Performed in a healthful, natural atmosphere, and involving moderate exercise for all, the game is a wonderful platform for family interaction.

In fact, there are few stronger catalysts for family bonding than golf, where each member actually shares the same "fascination."

As discussed later in this book, "family golf" could well be the game's "wave of the future."

I have a theory about why golf inspires such devotion to its virtues. I believe the game catches its players "naked,"—vulnerable—forcing them to think, perform, and react immediately and with no one to help them.

I also believe that people are basically good—and that a challenging situation brings out the best in them. Have you ever noticed that when everything's on the line, even normally selfish, rude people will band together for the common good?

I've found human nature to be kind, caring, and considerate. It's the incessant demands of society and our many daily irritants that interfere with these positive natural tendencies.

Golf offers us a wonderful escape from society's stresses; it's an excursion into Nature with the individual at the controls. Here, in a natural setting, rules, etiquette, honor, fairness, and courtesy begin to resurface, taking their rightful places—if only while we are on the golf course. But if we play enough golf, its virtues will surely influence other areas of our lives.

Let's go back over the list of golf's virtues. They include respect for rules, self-discipline, etiquette, responsibility, and self-control. Does this list sound familiar? It should, because it's a list of what's lacking in many areas of our society today. (Appendix II of this book outlines a new program called Operation Golfstart, aimed at helping inner-city youth by exposing them to the virtues of golf).

Golf can be a vehicle for tremendous social healing (as outlined in Appendix II, Operation Golfstart). It can also provide a great deal of personal pleasure. But what if your frustration level is higher than your enjoyment level? Are you missing out on golf's potential benefits in your life?

If so, it's time to explore ways to raise your enjoyment level and take advantage of golf's potential power to enhance your life.

*When we make full use of our senses,
our minds are better able to influence
the movements of our muscles.*

—Larry Miller

4

Discovering Golf's Magic

All of us, at times, become aware of just how far we are from reaching our full potential. Indeed, I suspect that this awareness is the silent cause of much human depression. For most of us, this fast-paced, demanding world leaves little time to put forth our optimum efforts. To overcome this problem, we need to adopt a more structured approach to achieving excellence.

Golf, by its nature, provides a fertile opportunity for us to achieve excellence, along with personal enlightenment and inner transformation. Since we usually play the game alone, even when we are in a foursome, there is plenty of time between shots for introspection. With countless variables to compute on any given shot, we have almost unlimited opportunities to think positive or negative thoughts.

Would it surprise you to know that the most exciting moments in golf seem to follow *positive thoughts* and end with *positive results?* This is the common thread linking every unusual experience I've had in golf or heard about from others.

For example, we've all heard bizarre tales of golf balls skimming over water, glancing off trees, or taking some other weird bounce and finding their way to the cup for a hole-in-one. Could it be that some special *positive energy* is the catalyst for these happenings? I strongly believe that this is the case.

I recently heard of an incident in which a player hit a shot to a par three hole and pushed the ball at least 40 yards to the right of the green. The golfer was yelling "Fore!" to the group on the next tee. One of the members of that group said, "Watch this. The ball will probably hit one of our carts and bounce onto the green." Moments later, the ball struck one of the golf carts, then glanced off the ball washer onto the green and into the cup for a hole-in-one!

Most observers of sports are aware of it when positive momentum is building in an individual or a team. It's in the midst of these winning streaks that we often see mind-boggling, record-setting performances. But when an individual or a team is on a downward spiral or in a prolonged slump, seldom, if ever, do we see the heart-stopping move, the special performance.

As I mentioned earlier, author Michael Murphy has probed deeply into golf's complexities, especially those involving the mental side of the game. He says that often he would experience a "special grace" while playing golf. The game seemed so *easy*. But then, just as mysteriously, that grace would leave without warning. Murphy also noticed the same thing happening to other golfers.

As he explored this mystery, he found it was actually possible to create the conditions essential for a transcendent experience. He theorized, in part after his long-term study of Ben Hogan, that "maybe you couldn't make the wonderful moments happen, but you could set the stage for them with proper practice."

Murphy's search for a method to integrate technique with thought and feeling brought him to the concept that the mind and the body are one. This, he knew, was the feeling he had had when playing his best golf. He also developed the idea that sports, including golf, can be a way to elevate ourselves to a higher dimension of experience—a kind of "Western Yoga."

How can golf be an efficient vehicle for human transformation? First, let's keep in mind what Shivas Irons, the hero in Murphy's *Golf in the Kingdom*, taught: "It's the living of these things that really counts, not the talking and the writing."

Before we can create meaningful change, we really have to want it. Only with a positive approach will we be open enough to take advantage of the transformative energies available to us.

Here at the Holographic Golf Institute, we have been using several techniques to help golfers tap into these energies. Our approach is to offer a package of strategies aimed at improving the *whole* person, not just the golf score. The best recommendation I can give for these methods is that I've consistently seen them work! I believe they will help anyone who applies them to his or her life.

These techniques include:

- golf as therapy for both physical and emotional needs;
- "soft eyes" and "the power of waiting"—techniques to improve our golf swings;
- the sound of the "swish"—how it can add distance to our drives;
- the power of mental imagery to create great shots;
- *Ch'i*—how to harness our invisible inner force; and
- being "in the state of flow" to create apparent miracles on the course.

Golf as Therapy

The field of "therapeutic golf" is an exciting new area that promises real breakthroughs in physical and emotional healing. At the Institute, we've developed combined approaches to help golfers with some of their most common bodily ailments, including lower back pain, tendinitis, and arthritis.

For instance, bad posture when addressing the ball can be a major cause of back pain, so we first make sure that the stance is correct for each person's anatomy. We then have the golfer take long, slow swings with a weighted driver. This stretches and builds the appropriate muscles safely and properly. The result is doubly beneficial: back muscles are strengthened and the shoulder turn is improved. Incidentally, all therapeutic practice sessions at the Institute include instructions on swing mechanics to maximize the golfer's performance.

We've found that practicing sand shots from green-side bunkers can work wonders for other types of pain, especially tendinitis. I once had a student who suffered a great deal from this condition. While we were having a session on the range one day, the pain began to manifest, so I told him to bring his sand wedge to the practice bunker. I had him dump about fifty balls into the bunker and then proceed to blast them out one by one, every ten seconds, to a flagstick no more than ten to twelve yards away.

It's important to note that the sand was fairly soft in texture, and every shot was played from a perfect lie which didn't require any digging. My student was encouraged to play these easy sand shots with a long, slow, flowing, rhythmic swing. As he continued practicing, his pain greatly diminished. The next day, there was no sign of pain or soreness.

I believe that the sand offered just the right amount of resistance to safely exercise the tendons, avoiding further damage to them while building their strength. This "treatment" has been successfully repeated often, each time with positive results. In fact, thoroughbred trainers often take horses with sore ankles for walks on the beach.

In the area of emotional and mental challenges, we are using a combination of therapies to reduce and eliminate stress, anger, and poor concentration. For example, students with stress and anxiety symptoms are asked to practice forty-five minutes of uninterrupted, thirty to forty-yard soft pitch shots. These shots are soothing. They require touch, feel, and rhythm, and are performed best with an unhurried, almost lazy technique. They are pretty shots as they float softly through the air and land gently upon the green. When performed in a pleasing setting, with perfectly manicured grass and trees all around, they can transport the golfer to another world—one far away from stress and anxiety.

We ask golfers to repeat this shot until they get into a rhythm, achieving a measure of consistency and control. When they reach a high level of concentration—usually characterized by consistent proficiency and a trance-like calm—we reinforce the exercise with verbal back-up applicable to their daily lives. This reinforcement usually involves pointing out positive aspects of the student's life situation, job, or hobby. For instance, we might help a car salesman understand that the customers he views as being demanding, or as time-wasting, irritating window shoppers, are actually people just like himself, who also have families and stressful jobs. We encourage him to see in these people opportunities to make new friends and to learn more about others.

We also help our students appreciate how each situation in life offers one of two different opportunities. One type calls for a logical, reasoning approach, while the other requires an intuitive, creative strategy. We insist on a practice program that helps instill the importance of achieving an ideal balance between these two abilities. Called "brain-balancing," it consists of practicing equal numbers, alternately, of routine, straightaway shots and creative, ball-maneuvering shots such as intentional hooks, slices, and low and high shots. By learning how to use both capabilities in a balanced way, the golfer develops mental versatility —a definite asset both on and off the course. (In the next chapter, we'll look at how the two sides of the brain actually work.)

No matter what the golfer's needs are, we usually play a round of golf together before beginning therapy. This allows us to determine the golfer's personality and to assess whether or not there is a lot of anger. If this is the case, we pick a hole that has both a following wind and an extremely wide, downhill fairway. Then, we have the person hit drivers over and over again. This builds confidence, while draining their aggression. We also ask the golfer to consider constructive thoughts, such as Shivas Irons' advice to be "the calm, solid center in the face of a strong headwind."

Golfers with poor concentration are asked to make three-foot putts. Although they are straight-in putts, there's a catch—the person must make fifty in a row. If the golfer misses on the forty-ninth putt, the process starts again. It's a great way to learn how to sustain concentration—as well as how to become a much better putter!

"Soft Eyes" and the "Power of Waiting"

Visualization is a powerful technique. In *Holographic Golf*, I described how it leads the mind to direct the body and how it must be cultivated through practice, just like any mechanical part of the swing. Visualization enables us to conjure up confidence-boosting alignments or scenarios that assist us in freeing our minds from doubt, anxiety, or other inhibiting negative thoughts.

One technique we at the Institute have found to be very effective in improving the swing is the use of "soft eyes." Golfers are taught to avoid staring at the ball too intently when addressing it. When they look at it in a general way, it promotes more freedom of movement, and the golfer avoids becoming what we call "ball-bound." We also tell students to avoid looking directly at, or dwelling upon the water, trees, or sand hazards. It's all right to be aware of these things peripherally, but we recommend concentrating more directly on *positive* locations for their shots.

Interestingly, this same technique is being used in other sports with equal success. An accomplished equestrian told me he avoided looking too intently at upcoming jumps because his anxiety could be transmitted to the horse. Not only could this influence the quality of their performance, but it could affect the safety of horse and rider, as well.

Author George Leonard describes using soft eyes in the martial arts:

> *"When you are attacked by four people simultaneously, you don't have time to see everything in sharp focus, but you must see movement and relationship clearly. Soft eyes*

provide a way of seeing everything at once,
being part of everything."

Another technique we use at the Institute also has a counterpart in another sport. It's the "power of waiting." At one point in his celebrated baseball career, Japanese home-run record-holder Sadaharu Oh developed a flaw in his swing. Oh's manager asked a martial arts instructor for advice. The response was short and simple:

> *"Look, the ball comes flying in whether you like it or not, doesn't it? Then all you can do is wait for it to come to you. To wait, this is the traditional Japanese style. Wait. Teach him to wait."*

Considering that it takes less than a second for the ball to reach the batter after the pitcher releases it, it's easy to see that there isn't much time to do any actual waiting! But the advice was aimed at getting Oh to avoid being so intent on hitting the ball that he would swing too soon and poorly. For years, the same admonition has been applied in golf. A cardinal rule is to *wait on the ball*, meaning "don't be too anxious to hit it." If power is applied prematurely, there will be too little of it left when the right time comes to apply it.

The Sound of the "Swish"

A few years ago in Chicago, when I was developing and testing the theories that led to the writing of *Holographic Golf,* I had an opportunity to see just how effective our methods could be.

Late one afternoon, after a tiring but energizing day of teaching twelve lessons, I was leaving the lesson tee and was looking forward to a quiet, restful dinner alone. As I walked toward the clubhouse, I noticed an elderly man coming toward me. He appeared to be at least eighty years old and looked rather weak. His walk indicated that he might have an advanced case of arthritis.

"I've been looking for you,"the old man said. "I understand that you're getting great results with your students and that you are a good teacher."

I thanked him for his kind words and asked him how I could help. I was surprised when he told me that even though he was eighty-two, he played golf four or five times a week and walked when he played. I never would have believed it. He then said he wanted me to show him how to get fifteen more yards on his drives.

Given the circumstances of his age, his condition, and his lack of strength, this seemed an impossible challenge. As I checked his clubs to see if an equipment change could give him more length, I had a brainstorm.

I had recently been experimenting with "sense enhancement," a method of incremental training that helps the senses become more acute. The same technique is used by martial arts *ninjas*, (highly trained specialists) to learn to actually "climb"walls using only their hands and feet. They start out climbing up an incline of forty degrees or so. Then the amount of incline is increased by one-thirty-second of an inch each day. This incremental training allows for a steady, yet almost imperceptible development in the ability to adapt to the angle. Eventually, ninjas can climb up a ninety-degree wall!

So I had my elderly student bring his driver to the lesson tee. First, I asked him if his hearing was good. He said he had perfect hearing. Then I asked him to hit a few drives for me, which he did. Although he made solid contact, they went no farther than 150 yards.

I then asked him to take a few practice swings with no ball. After a few of these, I asked him if he could hear the "swish," the sound of the club moving through the air in the hitting area (the area where the ball would be resting, also called the impact area).

He said, "Of course I can hear it." So I asked him to take another couple of practice swings, focusing his attention on the swish and trying to make the sound a little louder. After a couple of tries, sure enough, the swish became perceptibly louder.

Then I said, "That's really good, but make it just a little louder." So he did, after a few more tries. He was really swishing now. The sound was about two levels up.

All golf instructors know that distance comes from two primary factors: solid contact between the club and the ball, and the speed of the club when it hits the ball. The loudness of the swish increases as the speed of the club increases. And the speed of the club increases as the left-arm, clubshaft angle is retained farther into the downswing, yet released to square at impact. Technical stuff.

But making a louder swish is not technical at all. Even this frail, arthritic old man could do it. So I teed up another ball for him and told him to make the loud sound again. On his first attempt, he drove the ball 175 yards!

He turned around to face me, smiled, and nodded as if to say he understood what had happened. He reached into his pocket, paid me for a full one-hour lesson, and walked away. I never saw him again, which probably meant that he stayed happy with his drives. Since that day, I've always had a mental picture of him at some course just swishing away.

If I had tried to explain things like "holding the angle," or "late release," we could have spent many frustrating days on the lesson tee. I could have broken down his swing and analyzed it, but to no avail. The old man would have spent (actually wasted) lots of money. But because I knew about sense-enhancement and its connection with swing mechanics, I was able to help him make his swish louder and his drives longer.

The Power of Mental Imagery

Many people with medical problems are finding relief with the help of mental imagery, or visualization. Doctors and therapists are now training people to use their minds to mobilize the body's healthy cells, and then attack and destroy the sick cells that are causing disease. This method can get results with every possible condition, from a simple cut to a disease as complex as cancer.

Dr. Carl Simonton, medical director of the Cancer Counseling and Research Center in Dallas, Texas, is a pioneer in the field of mental imagery. Let me tell you about one of his cases to illustrate how powerful this technique can be.

A sixty-one-year-old man was diagnosed with throat cancer. His weight had dropped from 138 pounds to 98 pounds. He was extremely weak, could barely swallow his own saliva, and was breathing with difficulty. His doctors reluctantly decided to give him radiation therapy despite a distinct possibility that the treatment would only add to his discomfort without significantly increasing his chances for survival.

Then, to the man's good fortune, Dr. Simonton was asked to participate in his treatment. Dr. Simonton suggested that the patient himself could influence the course of his disease and proceeded to teach him a number of relaxation and mental imagery techniques that he and his colleagues had developed. From that point on, three times a day, the patient pictured the radiation he received as consisting of millions of tiny energy bullets bombarding his cells. He also visualized his cancer cells as being weaker and more confused than his normal cells and thus unable to recover from the radiation.

Then he visualized his body's white blood cells —the "soldiers" of the immune system—swarming over the dead and dying cancer cells and carrying them to his liver and kidneys to be flushed out of his body. The results were dramatic, far exceeding what usually happened when patients were treated solely with radiation. Not only did the patient experience no side effects from the radiation treatments, but all signs of cancer vanished in just two months!

Although Dr. Simonton has an excellent track record with cancer patients, the technique does not work as well for some as it does for others. The reason for this, I believe, lies not in the validity of the concept but in how effectively it is applied.

During one of our brainstorming sessions at the Institute, I discovered an innovative and highly surprising application of visualization. I call it "pre-shot self-adjustment." It's one of those paper-clip-simple discoveries that all golfers can easily and immediately use to lower their scores. Here's how it works.

Have you ever noticed that when you hit a bad shot or putt and immediately drop another ball, nine times out of ten you'll self-adjust and perform the shot correctly, the way it was intended? This is due partly to your taking advantage of the feedback you got from the first shot, and partly to the fact that the pressure's now off.

We use this insight by asking our students, before they swing, to visualize two consecutive bad shots—right down to seeing the ball landing in the sand or splashing into a water hazard. Or, if there's an out-of-bounds to the right, we get them to see *in detail* the ball slicing straight out-of-bounds twice.

Then, having "felt" the mistake through visualization, the students are told to visualize where they actually want the ball to go. Then, they swing.

This time, they will find that their bodies self-correct, and they will follow their minds' directions to hit the right shot. Having already mentally hit the two poor shots, they will produce an acceptable shot nine out of ten times and quite often, a very good one.

The key to the effectiveness of this technique is the individual's clarity of visualization, which can come from diligent practice. Just like chipping, putting, or any other golfing skill, visualization gets easier and more effective with repetition. One way to strengthen this skill is to do an exercise Michael Murphy suggests in *Golf in the Kingdom*. With your eyes closed, concentrate on seeing a golf ball in your mind's eye in complete detail, including the dimples, the name "Titleist," and the number. When the image fades or disappears, bring it back. When you do this enough times using any image you like, you'll have a highly developed visualization "muscle." And as this muscle develops, your success with visualization increases!

Ch'i—Our Invisible Inner Force

Mental imagery can be a powerful tool, both on the course and off. But it is just one of several inner forces that we can tap. Another one is our *ch'i*, the name used by the Chinese to describe the universal life force that permeates all things. This force can be controlled by uniting it with the mind and body through physical movement, breathing techniques, and meditation.

When we wish for something with all our might, we are using *ch'i*. This is a way of mentally focusing our energy, and it can be developed, with practice, to the point where it has a laser-like quality. A frantic mother may be using a rush of adrenaline to lift a car from her injured child, but it is actually *ch'i* at its most focused and highest level that directs this rush. Here's an example of how we can use *ch'i* in the golf world.

Arnold Palmer, one of the game's greatest players, went into the final round of the 1960 U.S. Open trailing the leader. He knew he needed a really low score to win and programmed himself for one of his classic, final-day charges. Wanting to make a statement to the other golfers, he was determined to get his closest competitor's attention with a spectacular start. Standing on the first tee, Palmer projected fierce determination. He seemed to be summoning extra energy from within, and indeed he was. Palmer lashed into that tee shot and drove the ball to the green of the par four hole some 340 yards away, far surpassing his average drive of about 280 yards. It was the adrenalin rush, prompted by his *ch'i*, that gave him the increased power.

The way Palmer focused his mental energy led to his summoning of "something more," which anyone can do with the right effort.

Here's a practical example of one way to cultivate *ch'i*. I guided my fourteen-year-old twin sons, both basketball fanatics, through the following exercise. To their delight and amazement, it immediately increased their jumping ability by eight inches!

First, I asked them to stand next to a wall and then to jump up, touch a spot, and mark it. Next, I asked them to try to jump higher. After a few tries, they leveled out at about what they believed to be their top height.

Then I said, "Now I want you to step up to the wall and stand next to it for sixty seconds. Close your eyes and imagine that all of the energy in your body is rushing to your legs. Feel the power gathering. Now look at a spot twelve inches above your best jump. Focus on it and jump while keeping your mental focus on that mark. If you don't reach that mark, I'll wager you'll at least out-do your previous best—easily."

Of course, they did. And you can focus the same mental energy and tap your *ch'i.* You can apply this focused exercise to hitting tee shots or to "honing-in" accurately on the flagstick with iron shots. Your clear, intense concentration serves to set up a connecting field of energy between you the golfer and your target.

Japanese baseball player Sadaharu Oh found out about *ch'i* while he was studying the martial arts training techniques of Aikido. In fact, Oh said Aikido—sometimes termed "the way of harmony with the spirit of the universe"—was the reason he was so successful at the plate. He explained that one of the first things a student of Aikido learns is to become conscious of his "one point." He described it as follows:

"This is an energy, or spirit-center in the body located about two fingers below the navel. While many martial arts make use of this center, it is essential in the practice of Aikido, which requires tremendous balance and agility, neither of which is possible unless you are perfectly centered.

I discovered that if I located my ki (the Japanese equivalent of the Chinese term ch'i) in the spirit-center of my body, my "one-point," I was better balanced than if I located it elsewhere. If I located my energy in my chest, for example, I found that I was too emotional. I also learned that energy located in the upper part of the body tends to make one top-heavy. Balance and a steady mind are thus associated with the one point."

I have made tremendous use of this Aikido principle in my golf teachings. In fact, it just might be one of the most important elements of effective technique. I teach it to beginners even before I show them how to hold the club or how to stand with proper posture.

When golfers put their mental focus on their hands, their arms, or their thoughts, the opportunity for a centered swing is minimal, at best. But when they concentrate on their "one point" as they begin their pre-shot routines, and keep their concentration there through the shot, they have a greater chance of remaining centered and of developing efficient centrifugal force. This centering ability is essential to any athletic performance, since balance is the cornerstone of efficient movement.

When golfers are top-heavy and upper-body-oriented, the swing becomes a hit, which sacrifices power and accuracy. One drill that we use in one-point training is to have students practice balancing first on one foot and then on the other. The ability to do this for any length of time is enhanced by mentally focusing on the one point. If the person doesn't do so, he or she will eventually become top-heavy and lose their balance.

Although there are many ways we can harness *ch'i*, the major methods include relaxation and letting go, emptying the mind of thoughts, concentration, breathing exercises, and rhythmic activity. Earlier in this chapter, we discussed how to apply rhythmic activity. In the next chapter, we'll look at methods of developing breathing and meditation techniques.

Even a casual belief in the existence of *ch'i* leads us to believe that there are other unseen energies at work in our lives. And the fact that we can witness the results of their existence suggests that we can also influence them just as surely as we can influence where we place our hands or where we look.

"The State of Flow"

Perhaps it is there, in the unseen world, that the energies combine to bring about the experience of playing in "the zone," that area of pure concentration in which athletes perform miraculous feats of skill. American psychologist Csikszentmihalyi calls this type of supernormal functioning "being in the *state of flow.*"

Michael Murphy, in *The Future of the Body*, writes of Csikszentmihalyi's findings.

> *Though flow. . .involves many human attributes, it clearly includes an exceptional type of volition. It is characterized, for example, by a marked concentration upon the activity at hand; by intrinsic motivation rather than a search for secondary benefits; by a reduction or absence of limiting self-consciousness; by a pronounced sense of mastery; by highly efficient psychophysical functioning; by positive moods; and by*

growth in complexity of the self. It breaks through to new levels of thought and behavior without social reinforcement, and perseveres without immediate rewards.

I think back to those special times on the golf course when I functioned that way. The scenario was always the same. I would be playing alone, usually late in the day, and I could do whatever I wanted with the ball. I had total control of it and could play any type of shot I wished. I did not have to think of swing mechanics, only of the result I wanted. Drives were long and straight, and iron shots would hunt the hole. Putts would drop with amazing consistency. Strings of birdies, eagles, longer-than-usual drives, and a very definite sense of mastery were common occurrences. More than once I recall laughing out loud, assuming no one was near, then looking around to see if perhaps someone was secretly witnessing the unlikely feat. I knew that something extraordinary was taking place, but I had no idea what to call it or what had caused it to happen.

Now, thanks to Csikszentmihalyi, I not only have a name for those special times, those altered states, I am also beginning to understand them. And what's really exciting is that I am finding ways to make them happen again and again.

In looking for a common thread between them, the first factor I found was the solitary aspect of being in the state of flow. Csikszentmihalyi says it happens "without social reinforcement." Almost all of my experiences occurred when I was alone, and the two instances when I was not alone were marked by a pronounced concentration that rendered me "alone," nonetheless. I experienced a pure, intense feeling of being totally in the present. When athletes enter this state, they indeed seem to be in a trance of some kind.

Many people believe that getting into the state of flow—or into "the zone"—is something that happens at random. This is simply not the case. Not only do special alignments occur that create this state, but we can actually invite and encourage them to take place.

Our first step is to look for clues. By that I mean we need to analyze the conditions that were prevailing when our special performances occurred—right down to the smallest point, no matter how apparently insignificant. If we keep a record of these details, we will eventually end up with a list of common denominators, and that will give us a head start toward obtaining our best performances.

The way into the state of flow is through a repetitive, rhythmic routine. Every movement should be performed with the same cadence—what I call the "trance of routine." Let me outline a sample pre-shot routine that you can use as a starting point. It's one everyone can adapt, using his or her own personal touches.

1. Line up the shot from behind the ball, looking down the target line toward the target. This view provides a better perspective for alignment and also offers a beginning point.

2. Pick a spot in front of and close to the ball, along the target line. You'll use it to aim the clubhead. It's important to be able to see this spot peripherally while you're addressing the ball. This technique gives you the most precise alignment and aim.

3. Place the clubhead down first, aligned with the chosen spot. The idea is similar to aiming a rifle barrel. In golf, the clubface is the barrel, and the ball, or bullet, starts from it. You must aim the clubface at the target.

4. Without moving the clubhead, grip the club and take the appropriate stance. If you move the clubhead, your feet will usually move to match

it. This mistake can result in poor aim and alignment.

5. Eye the target, flex the knees slightly, and get comfortable. Getting comfortable means feeling loose and reflexive. There should be no stiffness or tension, especially in your hands, arms, or shoulders.

6. Waggle the club for rhythm, settle into a good balance, and slowly start the swing. To settle into balance, many top players use a subtle rocking motion from one leg to the other. The weight gently shifts back and forth, and ultimately, before the swing begins, is pretty evenly distributed. Balance is synonymous with equal distribution. Many good players move their feet, shifting and lifting one foot and then the other as they prepare to play a shot. They are finding their stance, or seeking balance, as they get ready to swing from a balanced, settled, and stable yet reflexive position.

Make each of these six steps your routine for every shot and you will develop consistency and improved performance. This pre-shot routine also fills the critical time immediately before each shot with positive activity. Your mind has less time for the intrusion of negative thoughts, which can give birth to anxiety and tension, two leading causes of performance failure.

Getting into the state of flow requires a combination of positive factors, the kinds of activities discussed in this chapter and in the next two chapters of this book. It especially requires some form of meditative practice that will act as a springboard to prepare your consciousness, so your energies can align.

In the next chapter, you will learn how to align your energies in order to feel the special grace every golfer is seeking.

When we quiet the mind, the symphony begins.

—Anonymous

5

From Magic to Mastery

Now that we've looked at some of the special ways the golfer can improve performance on the course, what's the next step? What are the techniques we can use to evolve on our personal journeys? (Which, of course, will help us to improve everywhere, including the golf course!)

First and most important, we must practice all the techniques described in this book with a sense of enthusiasm and enjoyment. This is the best way to open up to their transformative power. Let's maintain an even keel and enjoy the journey, viewing every small difficulty or failure as simply another step toward mastery. As we move along, let's also stay open to developing our own techniques for incorporating these life-enhancing methods into our lives.

We're now going to examine four important practices that will benefit each of us, regardless of age, gender, or physical condition. These practices are meditation, natural breathing, optimum diet and exercise, and service to others.

Meditation

Meditation has been around for centuries and is found in many cultures. It is a discipline that creates a consistent, quiet awareness that can help body, mind, and spirit.

I began a daily meditative practice more than three years ago, and thanks to meditating, I've come to know a serenity that had been previously missing in my life. Meditation has also helped me to organize and prioritize my world. On the golf course it has helped keep me positive and focused. I can also stay centered throughout an entire round, something that caused me much trouble during the first part of my playing career.

The primary purpose of meditation is to help us awaken our spiritual consciousness. Quieting our mind and listening to our inner voice helps us in many ways:

- Our creativity is enhanced. Our thoughts and actions are reorganized;
- Our intuition is more fully activated;

- Stress levels are reduced. Our nervous system is revitalized, allowing us to process information from the senses more accurately;
- Our body's immune system is strengthened, encouraging our bodies to function more efficiently and speed healing; and
- Our aging processes are slowed, allowing older, long-term meditators to be mentally and physically younger than their chronological ages.

Here are some recommendations to help you get the most out of meditation.

1. Practice it daily, according to a well-defined routine.

2. Give importance to meditation as a process of opening your whole being so you can experience all its benefits. Consider setting aside a special area or room, a place free from distractions.

3. When you are ready to begin, sit up comfortably with your eyes closed. To induce the desired relaxation, you might begin with a prayer or any repetitive phrase (called a "mantra") that has the desired effect.

4. As you're meditating, try not to think of anything specific. When thoughts do occur, do not identify with them. Just *notice* them and allow them to flow through your consciousness. This is called "witness meditation." It is said that we reach our peak in

meditation when we no longer identify with our mental processes.

Most people who meditate do so for about twenty minutes a day. You'll find that this short period of quiet will consistently lead to a totally refreshed feeling after just a few sessions, and it shouldn't take long before you begin to experience many of the benefits of this practice.

By its nature, golf gives us opportunities to use many of the advantages meditation provides. We all know that we can display a variety of emotions on the course, from frustration and anger to excitement and joy.

After you've been meditating for a while, you'll observe that you are more aware of your mood swings. First, you'll notice the emotion *after* it occurs. Then, you'll notice it *as it happens.* Finally, you become alert to it *before* it takes place.

Meditation helps us to better diagnose the causes of our emotions and create strategies to eliminate the negative emotions while increasing the positive ones.

Breathing

Another important way to gain mastery over our emotions is by improving our breathing. If we breathe, we're alive! But what many of us don't know is that we can control the timing and quality of our breathing. An enhanced ability to breathe can improve our physical, mental, and emotional health and, therefore, our success in any endeavor.

Dan Millman, in *The Inner Athlete*, says the two emotions that stop us from functioning effectively—anger and fear—are both characterized by an imbalance in breathing. He points out that anger "is reflected by weak inhalation and forceful exaggerated exhalation. . . . Fear can result in very little breathing at all."

If we want to master our emotional states, we must begin to observe and then gain conscious control over our breathing. Our objective should be to make our breathing more *natural* at all times. This will help us automatically and rhythmically time our breathing to the cadence of both athletic and everyday movements, increasing their grace and ease. "Controlling the breath is . . . one of the ways we can exercise control over emotional reactivity, not by repressing, but by transcending," says Millman.

In order to learn how to breathe more effectively, we must, as with meditation, make it a priority in our lives. Our breathing exercises can be done anywhere, anytime, in any comfortable, relaxed position. But they must be done at least once a day to become effective.

Here's how to start. First, get comfortable, perhaps in a favorite chair or by sitting up in bed after awakening. Relax your shoulders by lifting and dropping them a few times until they just hang, letting you feel their weight. Close your eyes and your mouth, and touch the roof of your mouth with your tongue. Then gently tuck in your chin.

Begin to concentrate on breathing slowly and deeply, without any sense of strain. When you inhale, feel your belly draw downward and slightly outward. When you exhale, allow your belly to relax back up and in. Continue this conscious breathing exercise for at least ten minutes, always noticing the rise and fall of your belly.

After just a few daily sessions, you'll experience a pleasant rhythm and a feeling of being centered. It may feel so good, in fact, you may not want to stop! This healthier breathing will eventually become a natural part of your life, enhancing every daily activity.

Diet and Exercise

When it comes to our third practice, diet and exercise, I like Millman's statement: "If we don't take care of our bodies, where will we live?" It may sound logical to say that we should watch what we eat and exercise daily, but nothing is more vital to the quality of our lives—and our life journeys.

Although everyone agrees that a healthy diet and exercise are important, relatively few follow through on a regular basis, despite the strong fitness movement underway in our society. For many, watching television, having several cocktails, or engaging in their favorite sedentary activity, takes priority. But if our journeys toward mastery are to stay on course, we must emphasize good diet and exercise.

What constitutes the perfect diet is the subject of wide debate. Browsing through a bookstore you'll see many books with totally conflicting advice. To make matters more complicated, the best individual diets are as unique as fingerprints or snowflakes (or golf swings).

Basically, we want to have balance in our diets. They should include low amounts of animal fats, dairy products and sugar. But they should also include lots of fruits and vegetables, water, and fresh, unsweetened juices. Nuts and beans are a good source of protein, and fresh fish, especially salmon, is an extremely healthful food source. The goal is to maintain a healthy body weight while eating nourishing foods.

It's important to avoid overeating which will result in a heavy, bloated feeling that robs you of energy and can eventually lead to serious health problems. If you eat properly, you'll have a healthy, light feeling that will keep you energized.

Following an optimum diet, however, means little if you don't get consistent exercise. This doesn't mean you have to run out and join a health club.

Twenty minutes a day, every day, of stretching and fast walking will keep your physical body reasonably fit. When our bodies feel fit, we feel good about ourselves, and the effects snowball. As golfers we, of course, can also do a lot of healthy walking—rather than ride in a golf cart when we play.

Service to Others

The fourth practice I recommend—service and kindness to others—can be an incredibly transformative experience. Dr. Albert Schweitzer, one of this century's most famous missionaries, said that the only ones among us "who will be really happy are those who will have sought and found how to serve."

Helping our fellow man is really helping ourselves. Here's a little story to drive the point home.

A man died and entered the next dimension. An angel showed him around and led him down a hallway, stopping at a door marked "Hell." Inside was a roomful of starving, wretched, anguished people. They sat at long tables piled high with sumptuous food, but permanently attached to their arms were spoons and forks longer than their arms, which made it impossible for them to eat the food.

Then the angel led the man to the next door, marked "Heaven." Inside was exactly the same scene, with one exception: The people were happy and smiling, healthy, and obviously well fed.

The man looked at the angel with a puzzled expression and said, "I don't understand. What's the difference?" And the angel replied, *"These people learned how to feed each other."*

Golf is twenty percent technique and eighty percent mental.

—Ben Hogan

6

Performing at Your Peak

The golf swing is a two-sided activity. We hold the club with both hands, use both arms and legs, and pay close attention to the alignment and the workings of shoulders, hips, and feet.

Indeed, the ability to synchronize both sides of the body is vital to the overall quality of the swing. But what specific role does each side of the body play? And what influences the function of each side? More important, is it possible to enhance the performance of a specific side at will?

Our research at the Holographic Golf Institute indicates that the answer to the last question is an emphatic "yes."

We've known for some time now that each person's brain has a right side that largely influences creativity and intuition. The left side of the brain mainly controls the way we reason. Interestingly, *the left side of the body* is most connected to the functioning of *the right side of the brain* (the intuitive part). The opposite applies to the *right side of the body*, which correlates best with *the left side of the brain* (the reasoning part).

Michael Murphy pioneered much of the specific thinking that we've used in our teaching techniques at the Institute about how the brain works. He writes:

> *"All skill involves a certain measure of spontaneity and unconscious functioning. No one can create beauty, be it in a work of art or on the golfing links, unless he has both disciplined control (left brain) and the ability to let go to the sudden glimmer (right brain) . . . .*
>
> *Every shot has a conscious component and an unconscious one, a voluntary control and one that is involuntary. To know how to strike the balance is the very essence of golfing skill. The greatest champions, while having grooved swings to envy, come up with surprises that astound us. They pull off the unbelievable shot in the midst of contingencies too numerous to calculate. . . ."*

Holographic Golf introduced some innovative and effective methods to enhance our abilities to play better golf. But the Institute is now taking golf instruction to the next evolutionary level and directly influencing the degree of creative inspiration or steel-will discipline that a person puts into each golf swing. Our methodology promotes purity of concentration, the golfer's path to "the zone" or to the "state of flow."

During some research sessions at the Institute, we started filming players at every skill level as they practiced. What made the filming unique was that we zoomed the camera in very close and focused on the eyes. By simple testing, it was easy to determine which eye was a person's dominant, or "master eye." We discovered that many players used the non-dominant eye to look at the ball, rather than the master eye. When they corrected their focus, their results improved. But we went much further than that. As a prelude to particular golf shots, we started experimenting with "alternating eye focus." When combined with our suggestions specific to the type of shot required, we began to see immediate benefits.

For instance, let's say we have a shot from behind a tree that must slice (left to right) in order to land on the green. It is a shot that requires imagination, intuitive feel, and inspiration. *This is a right-brained shot.* Contrast this example with a straightaway tee shot to a narrow landing area. This shot requires disciplined, mechanical perfection. *This is a left-brained shot.*

Why invite the nonessential side of the brain to participate in the preparation and performance of a shot when no input from that side is needed? If the nonessential side is involved in deciding how to execute a shot, it can only confuse the process and reduce efficiency.

Many shots, however, involve some influence from both sides of the brain. The trick is to decide when to use which side. Now, here's the secret.

It's all done through the eyes. The eyes feed information to the brain which is influenced in its action by the visual data it receives. When the logical side of the brain is fed negative information, it can act in only one way—negatively. But when we send negative information to the creative, inspirational side, it will attempt to find a way around the problem.

Let's take a closer look now at our hypothetical shot from behind the tree. We've sliced our drive into the trees to the right on a medium-length par four hole. When we find the ball, we notice that it has a good clean lie in an open area, affording a full, unimpeded swing. The only obstacle, however, is a large, well-placed tree directly in our line to the green. Given the clean lie and a free swing, we opt for the deliberate slice around the tree and to the green, saving and perhaps gaining a stroke.

The situation calls for a right-brained, intuitive shot. If we allow the logical side to become involved with this shot in the planning stage and allow it to receive negative data from the right eye (looking at the tree that is in the way, for example), two unwanted things will happen. First, our muscles will be negatively programmed. Second, the focus will be shifted away from where it needs to be—on creating the desired shot and making it happen. More often than not, the result will be a jumbled mess, a confusing, hit-or-miss combination of information from both sides of the brain.

We have learned that we can actually send relevant information (such as visual data) to only the appropriate side of the brain for any decision-making process. This doesn't mean that the other side is shut down. The less essential side will still play its part in the process, but only when needed.

Here is how to handle this type of problem shot.

First, walk up to the shot and take an initial survey with both eyes. Then, assess the general picture and layout, and determine the distance involved. But once you decide to play the more creative shot, use only the *left* eye to visualize the shot you intend to play, right up to the time you address the ball. As you address the ball, however, shift back to using both eyes and execute your swing. Remember that by using only the left eye to visualize your shot, you feed information mainly to the right side of the brain—the creative, imaginative, problem-solving side.

Next, let's look at how you would perform a left-brained shot—routine, straightaway, and non-imaginative.

Assume you are in the middle of the fairway on that same par four with a perfect lie. You're about 120 yards to the flag which is in the middle of the green. You couldn't ask for a more straightforward routine shot. This is a shot that requires only disciplined, mechanical perfection. It's a shot for muscle memory, and it need not be muddled by any creative thinking. So you'll survey and plan this shot with your *right* eye.

When you address the ball, use both eyes only for "feel" and instinct. This way, your thinking will remain clear and to the point, just what you need for this routine shot.

Applying this alternating-eye-focus system to an entire round is simple. First, determine what kind of shot you have to make. Is it a creative (left-eye/right-brain) shot, a straightforward (right-eye/left-brain) shot, or a combination of both? Once you've made that decision, feed information to the essential side of the brain from the appropriate data-collector, the corresponding eye. Finally, perform what you've programmed, using all your senses as a sort of central guidance system.

We have been absolutely amazed at how much more effective our students have played when using this technique. One wonderful benefit of using this method is that we are constantly exercising and efficiently strengthening both sides of our brain as well as the corresponding body parts. This mind-body connection helps us to not only become better golfers but a better *whole* person as well.

Our work with students at the Institute using this method is also complemented by an exciting new process developed by Martin Sage of Austin, Texas. A brilliant combination of thinker and teacher, Sage loves to help people live happier, more productive, more enlightened lives. His Sage Learning Method uses immediate video feedback in a group setting to bring out the highest potential of each person's intuitive and reasoning faculties. Here's a brief description of how it works.

After everyone has been photographed and videotaped, the group looks at the various views of each face: head-on, left side (with right side covered), and head-on, right side (with left side covered). All members of the group say spontaneously what qualities they see in the face and eyes of the person being studied, such as sadness, contentment, wonder, and so forth. No opinions or stories are allowed—just one-word descriptions. These are the "before" observations.

Then each person is asked questions about his or her work and other interests. Watching the participant's face and eyes, the group identifies the emotional responses that indicate the participant's true inner feelings.

Sometimes a person's creative side may not be getting fulfilled or exercised, and this lack very definitely shows up on the left side of the face. The person may be a very creative, intuitive individual who is stuck in a mundane job but lacks the initiative to do something about it. However, when eight people in a group agree that they see sadness in the person's face—and he or she also sees it in the pictures—it's a powerful motivating force for action. One's inner needs are easy to deny in a one-on-one situation, but when eight people collectively agree that the message is obvious, it all hits home.

Sage takes each person's newly discovered awareness and helps him or her learn how to balance and fulfill both creative and rational needs. The result is a drastic reduction, if not a total elimination, of stress. The person feels better, looks better, and thinks better.

I've witnessed these results repeatedly and I've experienced them myself. That's why we have Sage-trained people on staff at the Institute. Like Sage, we use his method to help people make full use of their senses, thus influencing the movements of their muscles. They become better golfers and brighter, happier, more efficient people.

Two other "helping currents" golfers can employ to transform their performance is the use of music and poetry. Music in particular has long had a positive relationship with athletic performance.

Bobby Jones, golf's only Grand Slam winner and the game's consummate career amateur, has also written several books about the game's subtleties. Jones said he often heard melodies while swinging. When he was swinging well, he was able to time his swing to the rhythms in his "inner" ear.

During my years on the PGA Tour, I remember observing the music-golf connection countless times. Players would practice with headphones on and hum or whistle tunes as they played. All the while, they would swing their clubs with a rhythm and cadence that best matched the music. I've seen former Masters champion Ben Crenshaw, for example, playing with headphones on while listening to the inspirational lyrics of one of my own favorite singer-songwriters, Jackson Browne.

The Shivas Irons Society provides music on the course at its Games of the Links, an annual event at Pebble Beach. In 1995, bagpipes wailed the arrival of each foursome onto the magical seventh tee. Andy Nusbaum, playing in a foursome with Michael

Murphy, underscored the positive effects that music can have with a timely hole-in-one! Considering that the Society was inspired to provide the music from Murphy's suggestion in *Golf in the Kingdom*, it was a strange "coincidence" that he was there to witness the event. It was the first hole-in-one Murphy had ever witnessed!

I, too, had an oddly synchronistic experience with a musical connection while playing at the Peninsula Resort in Gulf Shores, Alabama, home of the Institute. I hit my third shot on the 628-yard par five second hole onto the green, but it was 75 feet short of the hole. The previous week, I had acquired Jackson Browne's newest album, *Looking East*. As I faced this monster uphill putt, I found myself humming the title song.

The putt was so long that one of my playing partners was surprised when I asked her to remove the flagstick. She was sure that I couldn't possibly see the hole from that distance, and in all honesty, I really couldn't see it very clearly. But I could sense the line very well. In fact, I felt as if some sort of connection existed between me, the ball, and the hole. It's a feeling I've had before with long putts— thirty-, forty-, and even fifty-footers. And when the feeling is very clear and strong, the putts go in. But a seventy-five-footer!

The feeling of connection to the hole was very strange, and the clarity of it was riveting. As I took a last look at the target before I stroked the putt, I really could not see the hole, but I could "feel" its location. The putt followed a track to the hole as if it were on rails. One playing partner said it went into the exact center of the cup with absolutely perfect speed.

And to top it all off, after my playing partners had finished putting, I walked back to pace the putt off to determine its exact length. As I stood on the spot I had putted from, I looked up into the rising sun and realized that I was, as in Browne's song, "looking east." Was it synchronicity or the alignment of positive energies?

I'm certain that my playing partners considered the putt to be a major stroke of luck. The logical left side of my brain would surely have concurred, but the intuitive side said otherwise. It said that something else was at work. I'm convinced that when a number of positive energies are aligned and then directed at a single goal (even sometimes unconsciously), what we call "luck" or "coincidence" occurs.

There's no doubt that our society believes in the transformative power of music. We hear it played everywhere, from courtside at basketball games to the waiting rooms of dentists' offices. And consider how much more we enjoy a movie with a good musical soundtrack.

There's obviously a place for music on the golf course, too. Music can be particularly helpful with your swing. Try practicing while playing music that really inspires you, excites you, or stirs your emotions. I'll bet you'll experience immediate improvement in both your rhythm and your swing mechanics. And as the swing gets smoother and more efficient, your game will become more enjoyable and your scores will begin to fall!

For those golfers who see things in a more scientific light, here's a simple way that music can be used to quickly tune up anybody's game.

Almost all weekend players, as well as most high-handicappers that I see, have swings that are much too stiff. These golfers usually lack a sense of rhythm. (And any good player will confirm how vital rhythm is to the golf swing.)

If you want to be more fluid in your golf swing, break your practice swings down into what I call the "three static positions:" the address, the top, and the finish. As you swing from position to position, use a musical three-beat count (one at the address, two at the top, three at the finish), timing the beat to the swing positions. You'll sense a rhythm to your swing and a cadence that will help eliminate any stiffness.

Golfers who are lovers of poetry—or other literature —can experience the same inspiration as do golfers who enjoy music. They can read rhythmic lines during practice or while playing. I know several players who derive great benefit from repetitive phrases they recite on the course. Any poem or writing with a cadence will help put you "in the flow," and it's all the better if it includes an inspirational message.

You might use your lyrical piece as a "golfing mantra," a tool to quiet your busy mind. Repeating one's mantra in stressful or pressure-filled situations often inspires concentration and realigns energy fields. I know one golfer who, in thirty years of playing the game, has never had a hole-in-one. On the tee of every par three, he chants,

"May the good Lord grant,
Before my golfing days are done,
That I might just once score
A legitimate hole-in-one!"

After thirty years, I think he needs a new mantra!

There are "helping currents" everywhere.
Stay open to them.
Search the Field to find them,
and when you do,
let your energies blend with theirs.

—Shivas Irons
and Larry Miller

7

The Ideal of Shivas Irons

Webster's dictionary defines "ideal" as the concept of "something in its most excellent form." Shivas Irons, the mystical golf pro in Michael Murphy's *Golf in the Kingdom*, personifies that definition. His approach to the game sets standards for excellence in two areas— the first relating to swing mechanics and the second affecting creativity and intuition.

Murphy's book was originally published almost twenty-five years ago but continues to draw thousands of new readers each year. It has become a sort of "bible" among golf's ardent followers, perhaps because those who really love the game see something of themselves—or something they want to be—in Shivas Irons.

Shivas wanted his students to ponder the mysteries of golf as much as he wanted them to celebrate the joy of the game, both on and off the course. Golf appeared to be his whole world, and yet he was able to recognize it as just a game. He would scrupulously record each stroke with strict adherence to every rule, and then completely disregard the score while suggesting that the student simply "smell the heather" or "listen to the sounds of Nature."

Shivas could play the game with a heightened awareness approaching religious fervor, but he could also engage in raucous barroom madness with the best of the party crowd. He could recite complex and obscure theories, and the next minute simply "listen to the insects."

Why is it important for us to examine carefully his apparently contradictory approach to golf?

I believe we come closer to the truth of how to really transform ourselves when we understand an idea once expressed by Pablo Picasso: "Art is a lie that someone tells in order to tell the truth."

We gain maturity, value, and depth in our lives when we are able to hold two conflicting ideas in our minds at the same time—and still function effectively. In writing, a phrase that contains two opposing thoughts such as "deafening silence" is called an "oxymoron." In life, an apparent contradiction is called a "paradox." If we look closely at our lives we can easily see that paradoxes, or contradictory conditions, are everywhere.

Golf confronts us with a classic paradox. It gives us the urge to master a game in which physical mastery is impossible. To the game's most devoted players, it is an art form of the purest kind. Indeed, as Picasso said of art, we can say of golf that it, too, is a "lie" we subscribe to in order to solve the "mystery of its unattainable mastery."

We need to develop the ability to embrace paradox while resisting the temptation to bring a sense of order to the puzzle. It is the only way life can teach us the profound lessons we need to learn. The English poet, John Keats, called it "negative capability"—the ability to refrain from attempting to shape the world, thus allowing it to shape us.

With this skill, we can penetrate some of the common barriers to our discovery of reality: our preconceptions, prejudices, and moods. Indeed, we can yield completely to the experience of paradox. We can then *become* the object we are contemplating, and embrace all sides of it.

Today, there is an increasing awareness and acceptance, even among hard-line traditionalists and skeptics, of the mystical and spiritual aspects of golf. The game's hidden meanings and teachings are being revealed through the daily experiences on the course of each and every golfer. During a round, a person's primary conflicts and tendencies are revealed. It's what's known as the "psycho-diagnostic level" of the game. Golf can be an X-ray of the soul, opening us up to insights and a kind of inner knowing about hidden aspects and meanings of seemingly ordinary occurrences.

The question that naturally arises, then, is: "Why are all these golfers keeping quiet about the amazing events they're experiencing on the course?"

The answer probably lies in something Michael Murphy calls "the strangeness curve," in which the number of reports diminish as the degree of strangeness increases. Based on years of research, his theory argues that people tend not to report occurrences that they consider strange or unexplainable, such as major synchronicities, because they don't want to be subjected to skepticism or ridicule.

But some noteworthy golfers *will* share their insights on the game.

In his book, *To the Linksland*, author Michael Bamberger offers golfer Mark Brenneman's best swing thought: "When I'm playing well, I can see the ball on the green even before I play my shot. It's like a movie playing backwards in my mind. The ball is already at its destination. All I have to do is make the swing. There's not a question in my mind. The only thing I see is the result."

Bamberger also tells of John Stark, a reclusive Scottish golf pro who is a mystical teacher and a philosopher of golf. Stark advocates concentrating on the *sound* of each shot, even on putts, chips, and pitches. He claims that a good, solid sound can be produced only by good mechanics. The more we produce that solid sound, the more often we will repeat good swings.

Stark asked Bamberger if he knew what it is about golf that "grips us so," then answered his own question:

> *"Because it gives us energy, Michael. That's the single best thing about the game. The better we play, the more energy we get. From now on, ask yourself, after every round, if you have more energy than before you began. 'Tis much more important than the score, Michael, much more important than the score."*

Writer Jeff Wallach agrees with this idea about the relative unimportance of the score and in his *Zen Lessons, Insights, and Inner Attitudes of Golf* he adds some other interesting thoughts.

"I believed that if I could only control my game, I could necessarily exert the same kind of discipline and control in other areas of my life. . . . The game was really trying to teach me the opposite lesson— to transcend control, to lose consciousness of everything. . . . Only then might I play—and live—purely. . . . When I stopped caring about such specific and limited goals as my score, when I surrendered to the process and just played, I began truly to experience and enjoy each shot, *and I began scoring better."*

Wallach says that golf, at its deeper levels, gives us the chance to get sudden flashes of insight about a subject that has nothing to do with the game. This can result in our seeing in a new way and eventually achieving true enlightenment. He adds,

> *"At this level, golf exists as a kind of golden circle, because the greatest teachings of Eastern philosophy—transcending conscious thoughts of good and bad, difficult and easy; living purely in the moment, without the distracting chatter of subjectivity —are the very lessons that can make you a better golfer.*

Michael Murphy, in an interview with golf writer and author Lorne Rubenstein, says that he believes that golf "can be a doorway into the further reaches of the body and soul. . . . The game produces this extraordinary intimacy, with yourself and others."

He then goes on to advise:

> *"Just remain present and attentive and let instinct, whatever you want to call it, do it. To use an old term from Native American culture, let the 'long body' do it. . . . The long body is a subtle phenomenon that golfers who have played in a state of grace are aware of—and who hasn't done that from time to time, even just for a shot or two?*
>
> *It happens, for example, when you are standing up to a shot and looking to the pin, and a powerful field gets set up with that pin. . . . (Ben) Hogan could even do it in practice. On the course you enter into that field, and you are now being informed along channels that are not ordinarily accessible to you. The golfer is 'pumped up,' or is 'in a zone' or whatever."*

When asked what he would say to golfers who want to transform themselves, Murphy replied that they should "step through the doorways the game offers. Search those soulscapes. If you do, you can be sure golf will present you with many, many surprises."

It is a tribute to the mystery of golf to acknowledge that, at best, most of us get only an occasional taste of success from our efforts, yet we keep coming back for more. Our small successes dilute our inevitable doses of failure, but it's clear that our fascination with the game is so powerful, we must keep on pursuing our mastery of it.

George Leonard describes mastery as "the mysterious process during which what is at first difficult becomes progressively easier and more pleasurable through practice."

The key word, of course, is practice. I always make a point of telling the hopeful parents of a promising young player that their child needs to develop a love of practice. It is the necessary ingredient in the journey toward excellence. Real progress is possible only when we commit to the long haul. This means, also, that we need to learn to love the inevitable plateaus that will occur in our learning cycles.

Shivas Irons had the right attitude about practicing. He turned the practice tee into his own personal laboratory, where he tested out all his theories. But he also loved practicing for its own sake, not just as a means to an end. As George Leonard points out, we need to see practice not only as something we do, but as something we have, something we are.

"The people we know as masters don't devote themselves to their particular skill just to get better at it. The truth is, they love to practice—and because of this, they get better. And then, to complete the circle, the better they get, the more they enjoy performing the basic moves over and over again."

The key, it seems, is the ability to *embrace* the practice. To love to practice assures enough exposure, and it is the prolonged exposure that leads us to the doorways that Murphy described earlier. When we practice long enough, we begin to feel the *subtleties*, and here the real fine-tuning of our games begins. But with inadequate practice, we generally go on groping forever—in golf and in life. Here's a story that illustrates my point about the value of repetitive practice.

A wealthy man who loved cats heard of a Zen master who was a highly regarded painter. The man asked the Zen master to make him a drawing of a cat. The Zen master agreed and told the man to return in two weeks. The man returned on schedule, only to be informed that the drawing wasn't ready. He came back a week later and many additional times over the next several months. Each time, he was told the drawing wasn't done.

Finally, after a year had passed, the man returned and demanded the drawing. The Zen master pulled out a pad and pencil and in about thirty seconds produced the most amazing and beautiful drawing of a cat the man had ever seen. The man was astonished, then grew furious. He asked why he had been kept waiting a year for a drawing that had taken less than a minute to produce. With that, the Zen master walked over to a closet, opened the door, and out came thousands and thousands of drawings—of cats.

Support for the idea of becoming totally absorbed in golf, whether we're playing or practicing, comes from Dr. Richard Keefe, an author and a leader in brain research. Dr. Keefe, who provided valuable input for the curriculum for Operation Golfstart (described in Appendix II), talks about understanding the Sanskrit term *nirvana*. Roughly translated, *nirvana* is the state of being free from all the cares and worries of life, and it is believed to occur when one reaches true enlightenment. Dr. Keefe studied many sources, but was still confused about the idea that life, itself, is the way to *nirvana*.

> *"Feeling resigned to my confusion, yet confident that understanding grows at its own pace, I went to play golf. On the course, I found that I embraced each event,*

each decision, each moment. I felt wide awake. My attention was snapped into focus on the details of the game. The grip on the club. The stance in the sand trap. The decision of how firmly to hit a putt. It had become clearer. These are components of bliss. Nirvana is not a dream or a fantasy. It is not an experience in which the angels sing and the sky opens up and God talks to us.

Those are images and symbols created in the attempt to communicate an experience that is beyond words. Nirvana is the full experience of one's life. It is everyday. It is what we do and who we are. . . . So it is with golf. The glory of golf is no more the final score than nirvana is the last breath we take before we pass out of our final life in the cycle of deaths and rebirths. It is the whole experience. Each shot, each divot, each unintended fade. All the putt-lines considered and not taken. The one booming drive."

Throughout this book, I have talked about all the ways golf can present us with opportunities to transform and fulfill ourselves. While each of us has a different expectation of our own unique potential, there is also the matter of human potential on a grander scale. With our supposed superior intelligence, are we as a species capable of circumventing the laws of physics? Will it ever be possible for man to fly? Or to breathe under water?

Now, as always, any real societal transformation must begin with individual efforts. Each of us striving for our own potential can build that momentum-at-large that will reach critical mass and produce global transformation. We can literally *force* positive evolution and streamline it.

By taking advantage of the communication technologies available today, what we do as individuals and in groups can involve staggering numbers of people. As the number of individuals moving toward enlightenment increases, I'm sure we'll see powerful networks of practitioners. For example, I believe we'll resurrect and emphasize concepts that will take on real importance in our schools, concepts such as mentoring and guidance counseling.

It's obvious, I feel, that our truest potential seems to be way beyond our everyday experiences. So it is fortunate that we are given glimpses, from time to time, of what we can really achieve, especially when we have high aspirations. But vital to realizing our potential is understanding these glimpses. We hold very real and accessible abilities that lie enfolded in a deeper order. By diligent study and deep involvement, we can together identify a path for positive personal and social transformation.

Humankind has taken giant technological leaps. We've bettered every single thing that we use. Why not better ourselves? Imagine the efficiency of a world in which each of us functions at our highest personal level!

Appendix I
"Deep Practice": The Benefits and the Pleasures

"To practice" means different things to different people. Most people will tell you they've practiced when in fact they've barely warmed up. I know a lot of intelligent, successful people who go to the practice range, hit a couple of buckets of golf balls, and go away thinking that they've put in serious practice time. And then they wonder why their golf game remains stagnant.

I'd like to tell you what real practice is. It's practice that is meaningful, effective, and lasting. It's practice that transforms.

Those of you familiar with long-distance running know about the "second wind" phenomenon. It's when you become exhausted and fatigued, and pain sets in—but you keep on going. And you go through the pain and exhaustion, right on through to another dimension of energy, a new level. This can occur several times during the course of a marathon run, and some runners say that beyond several stages of fatigue lies a dimension of "extra energy" in which you feel as if you could go on forever. But the runner who stops and gives in to the first wave of fatigue will never know the deeper levels of energy and the sense of heightened awareness that accompanies these levels.

Through practice we can improve, if the practice is real practice and goes deep enough into the activity to access the subtleties.

There's an interesting paradox here. We want to be able to perform on demand, right at the surface, yet that ability can be cultivated only by going deeply into the practice, where the awareness that will bring improvement awaits.

Here's the way it works: When you stand there on the practice range and hit 500 to 600 balls in a single session (taking water breaks, of course, and brief rest periods), you'll begin to *feel* the very specific, intimate subtleties in your swing.

At that point, you will be able to self-adjust effectively because you have become aware of the exact nature of your movements and of the club's precise position throughout the swing.

But—and here's the key—you cannot get to that level of perception unless you perform enough consecutive repetitions. You can't get there with only 100 or 200 repetitions. And so, like the long-distance runner, you've got to stick it out through the boredom and the fatigue. It's the only way to reach the deeper levels.

I extract a promise from every one of my serious students that they'll set aside a morning or an afternoon to experience deep, true transformative practice.

I tell them to arrange for optimum practice conditions: no distractions, nice weather, good turf, good balls, and plenty of fresh, cool drinking water. At this point, I suggest that they stretch and warm up. Then they're ready to begin the session.

I want them to hit at least 500 balls during the session, and I tell them that if their hands start to get sore, to put on a golf glove or Band-aids or tape, and then continue. Just as with meditation, they must stay with it.

Now, it's all right if they start with an awareness of special "swing thoughts" I've given them, relating to the areas we're working on in their swing. But what I really want them to experience is what lies beyond that. I want them to get to the subtleties, to the stage of heightened sensory awareness.

Only then can they achieve the improvements they're seeking. In fact, I'd like to share my principal doctrine for swing improvement: *Subtle adjustments to the golf swing can only be made when the subtleties of the golf swing are felt.*

Once golfers reach this level of awareness, they may find themselves "addicted" to the experience, as well as transformed. But there are no shortcuts to that higher realm. Only through the discipline of deep practice can one get there and it's a high that I would like every reader to experience at least once.

During this "golfing meditation," the swing itself becomes a mantra—taking the golfer into a rhythmic, trancelike state. As a teenager, I would engage in this "deep practice" regularly. So did most tour players I know. You, too, can get to the point where you'll *love* to practice, and that's how you'll excel—at anything.

And, if you knock long enough, the doors of perception will swing wide open.

The Stages of Deep Practice

Here is what you can expect to experience when you commit to a full deep practice session:

1. early fragmentation of thought, erratic performance
2. some sense of organization
3. boredom

4. fatigue
5. improved sense of organization
6. some efficiency
7. more boredom
8. more fatigue
9. better focus
10. deeper concentration
11. heightened sensory awareness and greater perception of subtle movement
12. effective self-adjustment
13. repetitive efficiency

Although by the end of the session you may be fatigued, you will also experience enthusiasm and well-being. This sense of renewal usually accompanies experiences of profound learning, or enlightenment.

Deep practice also results in your gaining intimate knowledge of your own techniques, which makes swing adjustments easier.

Appendix II
Operation Golfstart

As most of us know, many of the problems in our society—particularly in our inner cities—begin with those of our children. More young lives are being wasted and prematurely ended than ever before in our history.

Few of these children are ever exposed to rules or discipline and, tragically, many have little respect for human life. Their lives often involve dishonesty and violence.

At a golf writers' conference in Carmel, California, sponsored by the Shivas Irons Society, I asked the other participants if they had ever seen an eleven- or twelve-year-old avid golfer who was a "bad kid." The unanimous reply was "no."

Kids who are hooked on golf, even just a little, learn about its sacred rules and discipline, especially self-discipline. They learn sportsmanship and courtesy. They learn about honor. They become keenly aware of golf's etiquette. They learn respect—for their opponents, for the course, and for Nature. And they also gain self-respect. It's no wonder that many young golfers later become successful community leaders.

At that conference, I shared my plan to help turn things around for many of the youth in this country. My vision became a reality in the autumn of 1996 when the pilot program for Operation Golfstart kicked off at Douglass Elementary School in Memphis, Tennessee. Since the program's long-term success will depend on the support of many people—especially the kinds of people reading this book— I'd like to describe it in detail here. Afterwards, I'm going to share some of my views about another key component of societal transformation, the family, and how golf can play a role there, too.

Supported by the U.S. Department of Education and the Shivas Irons Society, Operation Golfstart will be offered to students in grades three and four. Children will learn the mechanical fundamentals of golf as well as its rules, philosophy, and values.

An integrated curriculum will enable the values of golf to be blended into the average educational experience. As a part of the regular curriculum, for example, math students might learn to keep a scorecard and add up players' scores. History students might research the history of local golf courses and the interesting golfers who have played there through the years.

Separate classes on golf will also be offered. They will be an hour long, two days a week, and will alternate between the classroom and the practice tee. These classes can be a new part of the curriculum or be a part of a physical education program already in place.

The program in each school will be coordinated by a team of volunteers composed of representatives of the school, local golf professionals, and business and civic leaders who are involved in the game. Each volunteer will probably contribute one hour a week to the program.

The more than 3,000 members of the Shivas Irons Society around the country will be instrumental in launching the program in their areas. I am committed to seeing that each program is properly structured, and I will also offer information to the program coordinators about the principles taught in *Beyond Golf, Holographic Golf, Golf in the Kingdom*, and *Extraordinary Golf*. My hope is that after the benefits of these school golf programs become obvious, other special educational courses on golf will be made available in other communities. This structured, guided approach will ensure a continuity of instruction in the values of the game. The idea is for golf's many virtues to become a positive influence in each and every student's life.

Equipment for the program in local communities will be donated by golf equipment manufacturers and suppliers, who are always eager to assist any undertaking that involves children.

I'd like to take the opportunity here to thank all those involved in getting Operation Golfstart underway, especially the members of the original Board of Directors of the program. Their input, guidance, and expertise helped keep the vision alive and well.

• Steve Cohen, president of the Shivas Irons Society and a former educator who has a knack for helping others find their true potential;

• Jesse Weeks, a fellow PGA member from Memphis and former educator whose determination and experience found the perfect home for the pilot program; and

• Richard Keefe, Ph.D., whose creative mind brought many important ingredients to the mix, including structuring of the integrated curriculum;

• Connie Bousquet, staff member of the Holographic Golf Institute and a registered nurse, who brought warmth, humor and insights into the program from Day One.

I've received inquiries about Operation Golfstart from people all over the United States who want to know how this program can be started in their own communities. The ball has started rolling, and my goal is to see that every school district in the country, and ultimately every individual school, has the opportunity to implement this program. Potentially, there may be millions more people playing the game in the future, many of whom might never have started without this initiative. What a wonderful catalyst for societal healing the game could be!

I believe in the potential of our youth to solve the problems of our society. I'm sure most of us would agree that anything we can do to reinforce the structure of the family would be a big boost, as well.

At the Holographic Golf Institute, we believe that when members of a family play golf together, family ties are greatly strengthened. Finding themselves in a natural setting, free from social pressures and distractions, they open up to sharing encouragement and praise with each other. There is no pecking order to worry about—everyone is equal on the golf course. Lessons learned from exposure to the game's virtues produce benefits for both the individual and for relationships within the family.

We offer family clinics at the Institute which include fundamental golf instruction, along with sessions in the Sage Learning Method and other forms of transformative practice.

The Institute is now working on an "extended family" program for those kids who have no close family members with whom to play golf. We also offer beginner seminars for families. Our hope is that the future golf population will be made up of a high percentage of families who began the game together.

We also encourage individuals to play alone periodically, preferably early in the morning or late in the afternoon. This allows them the therapeutic luxury of enjoying the game and the natural surroundings free from the anger and pressure that competition with their peers often brings. Too often, peer-structured games set up a competitive atmosphere, especially in the minds of those with fragile self-esteem. They create an adversarial situation in which hollow words of false camaraderie can hide a desire to dominate and win applause. Playing alone affords the golfer an opportunity to kick back and enjoy calm introspection.

If we observe a foursome of businessmen, teenagers, or housewives in the clubhouse after a competitive round, can we tell who played well and who played poorly? Easily, every time. But any one of those same people, when playing in a family group or alone, rarely gets angry. And if he or she does, it's a different kind of anger—less intense and shorter-lived.

When we play with our families, we seldom feel scrutinized, at least not judgmentally. After all, they already love us and we don't have to perform well on the golf course to win their approval. And when we play alone, there are no discerning eyes watching.

Playing golf alone or with one's family (biological, adopted or extended), produces positive qualities that help us evolve spiritually so we can find greater meaning in our individual lives and build stronger family bonds. These positive influences can result in creating entire communities of the same thread which, when woven into the fabric of society, can only make it stronger.

Appendix III
Eighteen Holes of Suggested Reading

To the Linksland
   Michael Bamberger / VIKING PENGUIN
— A great book about loving the game; it is also a wonderful golf travelogue about famous courses (and some unknown gems).

Breakfast at the Victory
   James P. Carse / HARPER SANFRANCISCO
— Subtitled *The Mysticism of Ordinary Experience*, this book shows us how to find the extraordinary in the ordinary to get more out of life.

The Seven Spiritual Laws of Success
   Deepak Chopra / NEW WORLD LIBRARY
— Based on Chopra's book, *Creating Affluence*, this book is a practical guide for personal spiritual fulfillment.

The Way of the Wizard
Deepak Chopra / HARMONY BOOKS
— Twenty spiritual lessons are given for creating the life we want. A great book. A must-read.

Zen in the Martial Arts
Joe Hyams / BANTAM BOOKS
— More on the mind-body connection, this book offers great stuff for golfers. We have much to learn from the martial arts.

Mastery
George Leonard / NAL-DUTTON
— This book shows that the real value is in the journey toward mastery, and discusses how best to make that journey.

Holographic Golf
Larry Miller / HARPER COLLINS
— This is the pioneering work on golf's new instructional direction.

The Inner Athlete
Dan Millman / STILLPOINT PUBLISHING
— A book about enhancing performance and reaching potential, this is great reading for any athlete, young or old.

Way of the Peaceful Warrior
 Dan Millman / H.J. KRAMER, INC.
— A mystical tale filled with practical life lessons, this is a particularly good book for those seeking enlightenment.

The Future of the Body
 Michael Murphy / J.P. TARCHER-PERIGEE
— The consummate, definitive study of human evolutionary possibilities, the book is also an exhaustive study of human supernormal abilities.

Golf in the Kingdom
 Michael Murphy / VIKING PENGUIN
— Published in 1972, this book is a continuing bestseller, a tribute to its vision. It is considered to be a "golfing bible" among those in the game's inner circles, an absolute must-read for any golfer.

The Psychic Side of Sports
 Michael Murphy and Rhea White
 ADDISON-WESLEY
— A terrific study, this book focuses on the mystical aspects of sports.

The Legend of Bagger Vance
   Steven Pressfield / MORROW
— A personal favorite of mine, this fictional tale is in the genre of *Golf in the Kingdom*, yet offers new ideas on the mind-body connection.

Links
   Lorne Rubenstein / PRIMA PUBLISHING
— A well-written, charming book about the lure of the game, it should be in any golfer's collection.

New Passages
   Gail Sheehy / RANDOM HOUSE
— An inspiring, hopeful book about life changes, it is good material for anyone on a transformational journey.

Extraordinary Golf
   Fred Shoemaker / G.P. PUTNAM & SONS
— This book provides a focus on how to enjoy the game more, and includes innovative practice methods.

The Holographic Universe
   Michael Talbot / HARPER COLLINS
— Here is an excellent explanation of the holographic theory, something we will be hearing a lot about in the years to come.

Agartha: A Journey to the Stars
   Meredith Young-Sowers / STILLPOINT PUBLISHING
— This book will inspire, inform, and change the reader. It answers many questions we all ask and is required reading for all my students.

For more information on the programs offered at The Holographic Golf Institute, write, call, or fax The Institute at:

> 805 Canary Pine Ct
> Mandeville, LA 70471
> (504) 845-0823 (phone or fax)

or contact us at our Email address:
http://www.downsouth.com/hologolf